LONG
IS
THE
WAY

Alton Hardy & Billy Ivey

ADVANCE PRAISE FOR *LONG IS THE WAY*

This is a beautiful, heart-wrenching and deeply inspiring book, the story of one man's journey through poverty, racism and despair. While uniquely his own, Alton Hardy's experiences are universally meaningful, laying bare not only the crushing weights of isolation, indifference and cruelty but also the healing power of kindness and acceptance from those around us and a God eager to embrace us with grace and love.
Dan T. Cathy, Chairman, Chick-fil-A, Inc.

God said to Jeremiah, "I am The Lord, the God of all mankind. Is anything too hard for me?" Long Is the Way is a vivid reminder of the power of God and the potency of His saving grace. Whether one is born and raised in opulent privilege or in abject disadvantage, no one is beyond God's reach. Alton Hardy had everything going against him. Yet, God redemptively worked through all this negativity toward a positive outcome—an outcome which continues to bear fruit for God's Kingdom—an outcome that continues to gratify Alton himself. For anyone discouraged by the current state of American Christianity, Long Is the Way is a must read. For all readers, it is a powerful reminder that God's redemptive purposes are invincible.
Dr. Carl Ellis, Provost Prof. of Theology & Culture at Reformed Theology Seminary

This is one of the most moving stories of grace I have ever read. The true story of one of God's special children. It is a memoir, a testimony, an autobiography, but it reads like a John Grisham novel. This book will awaken you afresh to the realities that must not be forgotten related to poverty, racism, brokenness, hatred, suffering, and pain. But it will also awaken you afresh to reality of God, His love, His power, His sovereignty, and His unfathomable ways.
Bob Flayhart, Senior Pastor, Oak Mountain Presbyterian Church, Birmingham, AL

This is an amazing book, because it's a gripping story about a remarkable man, written with unusual skill. I couldn't put it down, and I think you won't either. It opens our eyes again to the devastating power of poverty and racism, and the greater power of God's loving kindness. Thank you, Alton. Thank you, Billy. And thanks to all the dear ones who encouraged a poor, skinny, frightened young boy from Sardis, Alabama to see that he and others like him have great value in God's eyes.

Sandy Willson, Interim President, The Gospel Coalition

This is a shining memoir of reconciliation — from black and white to full Kingdom color. If racism is the new Goliath, as Pastor Hardy suggests, then Hardy is one of God's new Davids and this book his slingshot. I couldn't put it down and wept for joy.

Dave Beelen, former Lead Pastor at Madison Square CRC, Grand Rapids, MI

The Lord's anointing covers the life of my brother, Alton Hardy, through the way he leads, shepherds, and preaches for the glory of God. The story you hold in your hands is beautifully messy, difficult, heart wrenching, and soul searching. The hand of God working out all things for His glory and His children's good creates beauty from the ashes of a young man from Sardis, Alabama. You will see the hand of God protecting this young child from the poverty and violence of early childhood; flourishing this young man despite loneliness and lack of opportunity; and loving a young adult through hateful racism and prejudice. Ultimately, the Lord leads a man from Sardis to bring gospel hope to the urban areas of Birmingham, Alabama. I devoured this book. You will too. As you read it, you will find that the God who guarded Alton Hardy, will change you and give you His hope.

Herbie Newell, President & Executive Director, Lifeline Children's Services, Inc.

I dedicate this book to my friend, encourager, and wife,
Sandra my children; my late dad, Willie James Hardy;
my late mom, Verdell Hardy; and the entire Hardy family.

ALTON HARDY

For my children. I hope this story breaks
your hearts and stirs your souls.
I pray it brings you hope.

BILLY IVEY

AUTHOR'S NOTE

In late 2022, I was eating lunch with my friend, Greg Mixon—it was Thai food, if I remember correctly—when he mentioned that he had a story he wanted me to tell. I was mostly flattered, I think, but more than a little suspicious.

"What kind of story?" I asked.

"A true story," he said. "Alton Hardy's story."

I sat back in the cushioned booth, furrowed my brow, and grunted.

I had met Alton Hardy a decade earlier when he spoke at my church in Birmingham. I remembered hearing him and being moved by the earnestness with which he addressed the entirely white congregation. I remembered being moved by the courage it must have taken for him to stand alone in that place and lay bare his soul. I remembered his message. But I didn't know his story.

"Meet with him," Greg continued. "I think you'll agree that you are supposed to help."

A week later, I found myself sitting in the passenger seat of Alton's car as we drove the eighty-seven miles from Birmingham to Selma, Alabama. Tears overtook us both as he recounted the details of his childhood, as he patiently answered every question that popped into my head.

His voice cracked as we shuffled across the Edmund Pettus Bridge and he described the atrocities that occurred there decades earlier. He hadn't been a part of that fateful day, but like any good tour guide, he spoke eloquently and confidently about the details of March 7, 1965.

After four hours of talking and walking and driving and remembering, we were both exhausted and promised to get together the next week so he could tell me more.

And we did. Over and over again.

Each Wednesday morning for the next six months, Alton and I pulled up chairs to a wobbly coffeehouse table and talked about his life. Every detail. Every small story. I took a lot of notes and recorded mostly background noises on my iPhone, but the lion's share of this book is a simple distillation of those Wednesday morning conversations.

I am not a historian. I am not an expert on civil, social, racial, or human relations. I am just a storyteller who has been given the gift of a powerful story to tell. And that is precisely what this is. It is a gift. It is a powerful story.

In the interest of being genuine, Alton and I have chosen to use the authentic parlance and Southern, African American vernacular common to the place and time where and when these stories took place. Some of the names and titles in this book have been changed to protect certain individuals or organizations, but the details are true. The circumstances are real. And our intentions, as the writers, are pure.

This is an important and necessary story.

I am forever grateful that Greg asked, and that Alton agreed that we should tell it together.

BILLY IVEY
AUGUST 2023

"Long is the way and hard, that out of Hell leads up to light."

JOHN MILTON PARADISE LOST

SUNDAY MORNING, 10:00 A.M.

* * *

Good morning, ladies and gentlemen—brothers and sisters. My name is Alton Hardy, and it is a great honor to speak with you all today. I'm going to share something with you that is not only near and dear to my heart, but, I believe, is also dear to the heart of God. Pray with me as we ask for His help today and every day:

Lord, your ways are higher than our ways. And your promises are true. Your Word reminds us that "You saw us before we were born. Every day of our lives was recorded in your book. Every moment was laid out before a single day had passed," and we praise you for that today. Be near to us now as we dig deeper into this great story you have been writing to us, for us, with us, and for our good. Thank you for your mercy and grace. Come, Holy Spirit, and be with us now. It is in your wonderful, glorious, magnificent, and matchless name that we pray.

Amen.

The story I am about to tell you is true. It is my story. It is not an easy story to tell, nor is it going to be easy to hear. But it is a God story. So, it is therefore a story of hope.

CAN ANYTHING GOOD COME OUT OF SARDIS?

About six miles northwest of Montgomery, Alabama, near the town of Wetumpka—which happens to be pronounced exactly as it is written—the Tallapoosa and Coosa Rivers meet to form a waterway known as the Alabama River. It's a beautiful stretch of water teeming with largemouth, spotted, striped, and white bass; crappie, catfish, and snakes. Lots of snakes. But we don't talk much about those around here.

"Snakes," my grandmother used to tell us, "are the devil's helpers, and they out for no good. Some peoples say they is good'uns and they is bad, but I ain't never met no good devil, hab mercy …" Mama Fat ended most of her sentences with "hab mercy," but especially when she got riled up about something. When talking about snakes, for example, she could "hab mercy" so hard, she'd nearly pass out.

I grew up four miles as the crow flies from where that river cuts through Selma, Alabama, and the Edmund Pettus Bridge connects one side of the tracks to the other. If you walk the dirt and gravel roads that link farms to plantations to town, it's more like eighteen miles, but we hardly ever took the roads. It wasn't altogether safe to be on the main throughways where I come from, but especially the ones that hadn't been paved yet.

Those roads still aren't paved.

I was born exactly sixteen months after "Bloody Sunday," when the Pettus Bridge became famous and the Alabama River suddenly became more than a thread of water connecting Wetumpka to Mobile Bay. It was on that bridge and over that water where activist John Lewis and 600 marchers were stopped from crossing on their way to Montgomery. They were turned around, chased, beaten, and some were even arrested for walking with their neighbors that day.

The story goes that the group had planned to walk from Selma to Montgomery so that they might bring attention to the fact that Black people were being denied the right to vote. It didn't take long, though, for state and city officials to let their disapproval be known—loud and painfully clear.

Seventy-two men and women were hospitalized that day, and hundreds more injured at the large and far-reaching hands of Jim Crow.

It was reported at the time that no place in the South has felt the grip of Jim Crow tighter than Dallas County, Alabama. And that's precisely where I was born—smack-dab in the middle, but a whole world away from the Civil Rights Movement.

My family was not a part of Bloody Sunday. In fact, I don't think they even knew it was happening. That day, and that place, would become infamous and talked about worldwide for a generation, but we never even heard a whisper.

It can be hard to hear when you're being choked out.

My people's people come from Sardis—a beautiful, but nothing place as flat as it is empty. Though it's only a few throws of a stone from Selma, Sardis can hardly be found on a map. Aside from the crops that grow there—cotton, corn, hay, sugarcane, and soybeans from time to time—this place has no value at all.

Certainly no reason to be on a cartographer's to-do list, that's for sure.

My parents were cotton-pickers like their mothers and fathers before them, and so on and so on, and so it goes here in south Alabama. Our cotton days date back to when my people were wholly owned by the ancestors of the bosses we worked for a century later. These days, folks refer to what my parents did for a living as "sharecropping," but I'm here to tell you that we didn't share none of those crops. And you can hardly call what they did every day "living."

When I was born in 1966, Verdell—most people called her Belle—and Willie James Hardy had already welcomed eight kids to their shotgun house consisting of two bedrooms, a keeping room, which was exactly that—a room where they kept things—and a small, makeshift kitchen with a wood burning stove. This tiny shack was called Mr. Smith's place after the man who owned the land. It was positioned catty-cornered to a county dump, approximately three miles away through woods and fields from the land where my parents and siblings worked every summer.

I was birthed in that house in the hottest heat of the summer. Monday, August 8. I wish I could recall the looks on the faces of my parents and siblings as I came into that tiny place screaming my skinny head off. I imagine there was some joy in that room, but probably a lot more "Here we go agains" as they looked around and wondered, *Where are we gonna put this one?*

Winters are mild in Sardis, but only as it relates to weather. With no harvest to reap, it's a wonder we ever made it to spring when planting began. Summers are when everything happens, but the heat leans toward the unbearable, with air thick like an exhale from Satan himself.

And that's when the pickin' happens, in the summer. It has been said that Mama was back in the field on the Tuesday morning after I was born. That's just the way it was. If you didn't work, you didn't eat, and Belle had ten mouths to feed, including her own.

I started exploring Sardis when I was around five years old. I was too young to work the fields, so I'd just walk. And walk. And walk. I'd wake before the sun when the others were readying for the brutal monotony of their day, and simply step out into the bigness around me. It was cool in the mornings, even in the summer. Shirtless, and more often than not, shoeless, I'd shakily head out the back door and sneak through the trees that served as a natural barrier between our place and the empty fields behind it.

The area around our house was a vast wilderness. A ghost town dotted with squared-off parcels of land that connected corn to melons to beans, and, of course, cotton. Beyond the fields, though, that's where the adventure was. That's where animals lived: squirrels, possums, foxes, chipmunks, wild dogs, hogs, mice, rabbits, and birds. So many birds. I'd talk to the birds when I was walking. That was the only time I would ever say much of anything.

I was almost five years old before I started using words to express myself, and when I did, I had an awful stutter. M-m-m-m-my n-n-n-n-name … My name … i-i-i-i-i-ssss … Al-al-al-ah-ah-aaahhhhlllton. My name is Ah-ahl-ton.

It was pathetic. I was pathetic. I never even wanted to talk to myself. But I talked to the birds.

I was extremely slow in developing. I didn't even start walking until I was four. My family all thought I was simple-minded, or at least a little brain damaged. My father started hitting my mama around the time she got pregnant with me. Maybe he knocked her down or punched her stomach during one or a few of their scrapes. Regardless, the assumption for those who knew me back then was that I was an "unfortunate."

I'm not sure if my slow development was a blessing or a curse. I know for a fact, though, that it allowed me to stay out of the fields more than my brothers and sisters. When I was very young, they would carry me with them or strap me to their backs with an old sheet or pillow sack. As I got bigger, they'd just leave me at home. Alone.

Now, there's a difference between being alone and being lonely. I was both, to be sure, but there was something about being outside—in the woods—that made me not so lonely.

So, as soon as I was able to put one foot in front of the other, I took my loneliness to nature and wandered and wondered by myself. Talking. Watching. Searching. I can't fully articulate what I was looking for in those woods—along those paths and river's edge—but I never felt closer to finding it than when I was walking.

It was a daily search for meaning, I suppose. A longing for a Promised Land that I could not comprehend except when I was out there. I was in solitude by default. I had nothing but what God chose to show me in His creation.

Like the trees.

I studied the trees around me: how they reach upward and outward at the same time. Where they grow and when they flower.

*Leaves are larger on trees that grow nearer to a
water source. Smaller leaves and a sparse canopy means
we didn't get a good spring rain.*

I would study alternate and opposite leaf patterns as closely as I would study the beetles and dragonflies and earthworms.

Early in the mornings, there were flowers that would open up right before my eyes if I looked at them long enough. I was amazed at creation and all of the thousands of beautiful, amazing, intricate, and mind-blowingly simple things I would see every day.

But I never felt a part of it. I was just in it. Alone, yet surrounded by all of these wonderful things. Even still, I was hopeless. I had no ambition. No picture of the world away from the world that met me every day.

Hopelessness is having no identity, no direction, no understanding of belonging. In Sardis, my life was a picture of hopelessness. I didn't know what hope was, so I couldn't manufacture it. And I wasn't smart enough to counterfeit it. I was not even desperate for it. I was nothing.

* * *

My brothers used to act surprised when I would come home latein the afternoon as the sun set.

"I thought you was too dumb to find your way home," they'd laugh. "One of these days, you're gonna walk off that bridge and not be able to swim your way out, Alton."

They weren't wrong. I couldn't swim until I was twelve.

Some days, I wouldn't go exploring. I would go on a mission to find food. We weren't starving in the extended bellies way you see in footage from Africa or Auschwitz, but we were malnourished and hungry, to say the very least.

I would scale the mounds of trash and refuse at the "dobbage dump"—I couldn't say the word "garbage"—and dig through it for my breakfast or lunch. It wasn't all that bad, to be honest. You'd be amazed at some of the things people throw away: unopened cans of beans, tomatoes, and soup; just barely expired bread; boxes of cereal; potato chips; and a lot more. One time, I found an entire bag of Honey Buns. You'd have thought I discovered a treasure of solid gold. To me, it was even more valuable. I loved Honey Buns. Still do.

When the bounty was rotten, inedible, or there simply wasn't anything to be found, I would walk the fields and eat watermelons, apples, peaches, and corn. And grasshoppers. Somewhere along the way, I found out that grasshoppers were healthy to eat. I don't know where. But I ate 'em. Every chance I got.

I called them "hoppergrasses" growing up.

I still forget and confuse folks when I talk about how delicious a hoppergrass could be early in the morning.

My sister, Toni, would walk with me sometimes. We'd eat hoppergrasses together. For as long as I can remember, Toni has been my most consistent caregiver. She was never one for nurture, but she made sure I had what I needed to survive. "You can eat a lot of things out here, Alton," she'd say, pointing out a bush, flower, berry, or mushroom.

"You don't always have to be hungry, little man." She smiled. "See them white flowers? You can eat those. Them berries on that bush is good, too. But only the purple ones. Stay away from the red. They ain't poisonous, but snakes likes them, and you know what Fat says …"

"*Ha-ha-ha-ha-hab mer-mer-mercy!*" I interrupted.

Toni laughed and laughed. Oh, how I loved making her laugh.

It was Toni who showed me how to make a mud pie, too. Yes, a mud pie. In Sardis, and I assume other places, there's a certain red dirt that is sweet to the taste. It's a fine, velvety dirt you can find on the side of hills and on the banks of creeks and rivers. When you can find that particular red dirt, you're in for a treat. Pick the wrong stuff, though, and you're in for a gut-thundering stomachache for days.

Most days while walking, I wouldn't see another human being at all. I was a five-year-old little boy, alone in the wilderness—walking the rutted-out roads that connected to other rutted out roads that led to nothing—my everything.

* * *

At night, my father would beat the hell out of my mama. There's no easy or appropriate way to say that. He'd beat the living hell out of her. To be fair, it wasn't every night, but a peaceful evening in our home was much less likely than a throwdown.

My older brothers and sisters knew better than to be in the house when my father would get home. He'd come in the door all wound up, ready to explode, and my mama would meet him—shoulders back and chin outstretched—as if daring him to "bring it on." My mama was a strong and strong-willed woman. She never got more than a second-grade education, but she was smart enough to know that backing down and begging him to stop would only fuel his hate. The stronger and more defiant she could be, the less likely he would be to actually kill her ... this time.

My father was not a big man—maybe five-foot-nine-or-ten, and skinny as a rail. But he was stronger than a man twice his size, and tougher than ten. He grew up within spittin' distance from Mr. Smith's place, and like me, found himself alone by the age of five.

My father was then taken in by a large family near the center of Sardis and was made to work their entire farm, all before his sixth birthday. He was physically and sexually abused his entire life—repeatedly beaten by the men in the family and raped over and over by the women. That was his life, every day, until he left that farm at the age of eighteen, married my mother, and declared a role reversal.

Now, he was in charge.

You're never really in charge, though, when you are beholden to others for survival. He found himself begging for work on Mr. Smith's land, and that's where my family worked day in and day out. My father never had a special skill to speak of, but he had the uncanny ability to learn, and could convince just about anybody that he was an expert in whatever he wanted them to believe: farming, sharecropping, small engine repair, moonshining, grave-digging …

"You can't just dig a hole in the ground and put a body in it. You gots to know the earth. Soft clay can take a full day to dig, but rocky ground gonna take maybe three." He would say things like this having never even dug a grave.

He had no formal education and didn't have a vast vocabulary, but when he talked, people believed him. He was just gifted that way, I suppose. The words might have been Old South African slang, but he was college-smooth when he spoke them.

And so, he started digging graves. And that's how he started making moonshine, too. He just decided to.

The moonshine years. That's when the fighting and beatings really started to enter our home.

More often than not, their fights would end with Mama running away, but sometimes my father would simply tire out, exhausted from the kicking, swinging, and screaming at the top of his lungs. After he would allow himself to pass out, we would watch as Mama covered him with a blanket where he laid. Then, she'd drift off to sleep, lullabied by the throbbing in her head, chest, and face.

When the moonshine hadn't fully kicked in and he wouldn't stop hitting her, Mama would run out the back door and into the woods. He'd chase her, stumbling after her and swearing that he would stomp her dead if she didn't stop running. Mama spent more nights than we can count hiding, crying, sleeping in the woods, or under the protection of gravestones a few miles away. She knew my father would never go into the cemetery at night.

That's when the ghosts came out. Apparitions. Spirits. The undead. Whatever you want to call them.

We called them "Hanks," for some reason. I'm fairly certain it was supposed to be pronounced "haints," which, I have learned, are spiteful ghosts that look to steal things or harm naughty children, but as for me and my house, they were Hanks.

You can go back hundreds of years and hear story after story of Black people in the South talking about seeing ghosts, being visited by spirits, warning against voodoo, and ceremoniously fighting back dark magic with good magic. It's a cultural thing. But it's also a very real, very common, and very current thing—especially in places where massacres happened or injustice prevails.

Well, it just so happens that one of the bloodiest battles of the Civil War in the state of Alabama happened right in my childhood backyard, which is to say, in the fields of Sardis. The battle of Selma, a part of Wilson's Raid, saw a loss of more than 3,000 soldiers, combined, and sometimes those soldiers don't stay dead, if you know what I mean.

Mama knew that my father—drunk or not—would never go chasing her amongst the Hanks that showed up beyond our woods.

✳ ✳ ✳

The last time my parents ever fought in front of me, I couldn't have been more than six years old. I was very sick. I had a fever, and I recall being sore to the touch. My skin hurt. Even my hair seemed to have nerves exposed to the heavy air. The slightest touch would send me into excruciating fits of suffering. The lymph nodes under my arms, in my neck, and even in my groin, were bulbous and swollen.

But I was desperate to be held. Desperate to be loved and cared for by my mother. I was screaming and crying and begging to be picked up—in spite of the pain it would cause. I was covered in snot and sweat, tears and urine and feces. My mother was so tired—from working, from worrying, from more than likely not eating for days—from life itself.

And then he came in the door.

He was drunk and loud and angry at nothing in particular. At everything. Mama tried to calm him and begged him for peace:

"Look at Alton," she sobbed. "He's sick. He don't need this tonight!" Her words just made him angrier. He glared down at me on the floor and then let out a primal scream followed by a violent attack. He threw her to the ground and started kicking her—right next to me as I cried, arms still outstretched, still begging to be held.

My brother, Frank, was sixteen years old and watched this happen. He was a quiet kid—always focused on what he was doing. He never said much, but you didn't really have to guess what he was thinking. His eyes told you. He was a hard worker and had the confidence of our father, but he was built like our Mama—tall, big across the shoulders, and he never shied away from a fight.

The next night, Frank met our father at the door of the house and pointed a gun at his face. "You're not gonna hit Mama no more," he said. "You ain't hittin' nobody." Frank was not backing away as my father walked toward him.

"Boy, you better shoot me dead. Have you lost yo' mi—"

The words hadn't even left his mouth when Frank pulled the trigger and immediately dropped the gun and ran out the back. He missed. The bullet zipped right past my father's head and through the front door behind him, leaving a baseball-sized hole. Without hesitation, my father picked up the gun and charged out after Frank, emptying the chamber until the clicking of the hammer told him there were no more bullets. Frank was safe among the pine trees and under the cover of a moonless sky, but those bullets fractured our family even more. Frank never slept in that house again.

My father didn't come around much after that. I'm not sure if he just grew tired of the routine, or if Mama finally got the courage to kick him out, but from that night on, I only saw him in Selma. He lived in a big, green house next to the railroad tracks with six or eight other people. He would invite me and my brothers and sisters to come see him every now and then, but nobody much cared to spend time with the person who broke our Mama—literally and figuratively.

My father certainly wasn't the first hustler to come out of Sardis, Alabama, but he was probably the most creative. It's been said that he's been shot at more than a bullseye, but nobody ever made a mark. When he wasn't sharecropping, he was moonshining, selling stolen lawn mowers, digging graves, and, yes, most likely dealing drugs. The now infamous sheriff of Selma, Mr. Jim Clark, knew my daddy by name, and more than once came upon him making his moonshine. He and his deputies would, of course, arrest my father and throw him in jail for a day or two, but not before beating him close to death and making him drink until he couldn't make words. Those tactics didn't derail Willie James Hardy, though. A day later, he'd be back out there. Making moonshine. Hustlin'.

He was good at so many things. If he had been born in a different place, at a different time, he could have been the world's greatest salesman. He could have run companies, owned beautiful houses, driven fancy cars, and worn nice suits. He could have given us—all of us—anything and everything we could have ever wanted. He was that special. He was that focused. He was that talented. But he was born in Sardis. The son of a sharecropper, the son of a slave. I learned recently that my father worked the Smith land for twelve years without ever getting paid. The overseer always found a reason to not give my father wages: *You didn't clear; you weren't fast enough; you put the bushels too close together; you worked the wrong plot; you didn't work long enough; you took too long. What are you gonna do with money anyway, nigger? What do you need that you don't already have?*

It was after twelve years of this that my father finally lost hope. He turned to drinking. He turned to womanizing. He turned to hustling. He turned to beating my mama. He turned into something altogether inhuman.

I do not give my father free reign over the evil that he became. I certainly do not give him a pass for the awful things that he did. I do not forgive the way he treated my mother. But, looking back, it grieves me to say that I understand. When everything is taken from you—when you have nothing and are desperate for something, anything to make you whole—perhaps reaching out with clenched fists, or grabbing hold of a bottle is the only way to own something, if only for a single, bloody, painful moment.

* * *

My mama would moan a lot after my father left. Day and night. Tears would come, but it was deeper than that. Sometimes, it was like singing, but there was always sorrow in her groans. I've seen old movies that depict slaves in fields moaning and singing while they work. Sometimes, the songs have words, but mostly it's just a bellowing—like crying out in pain, with melody. That's what

Mama did all the time. We were hungry a lot after my father left. Mama would rock back and forth and moan and weep and beg the Lord—or whatever spirit she decided to call on that day—to provide food for her kids. And he did. More often than not, it came from the dump, but it didn't matter.

"You see this fruit?" She'd hold up a half-rotten apple or a handful of pecans someone picked off of the ground. "You better be thankful of dis here apple. God done give it to you, so you better eat it."

Manna from heaven? I suppose. It was food. But did the Creator of the Universe really just provide this rotten apple? Did He even know Sardis existed?

My mama hardly ever smiled. And I never, ever heard her laugh. She was six feet tall—significantly taller than my father—and hard as granite.

She had this way about her—this way of saying things and you couldn't tell if she was angry, happy, confused, or sad. It didn't matter. You just did what she said. We all did.

*   *   *

"We gon' get you baptized," she said one day as she walked outside, past me and my brothers.

Baptized? What does that even mean?

We had no idea. Andre, Vernon, and Charles protested when she said we would be dunked in the water on Sunday morning, but I was excited.

"Come Sunday mornin', y'all 'got be diff'rent," she said, looking back over her shoulder.

Different. That sounds just fine by me.

Mama didn't even know what it means to be baptized. She just knew it was part of the process … to become different.

After my father left, we moved from Smith's place, even further into the center of Sardis. Further into the void. There was an abandoned shotgun house next to the road that folks called the Cade Collins house. I don't know who Cade Collins was, but it seems he hadn't been much better off than us. The house was another three-room, but the roof was made of four sheets of metal. At least Smith had shingles.

Cade Collins was closer to Mama Fat and other extended family—aunts and uncles—so it was a good move for us. And it was just down the road from East Salem Baptist Church. East Salem is a tiny, white, wooden church that holds about forty people. When Belle Hardy and her kids showed up, folks had to stand in the back. The baptismal pool was a concrete tub that stood about five feet square and three feet deep. It was filled with water from the creek that ran between the church and the cemetery—the very same graveyard Mama used to sleep in, hiding from my father.

Reverend Short was the pastor back then. He was a tall, skinny man. The irony of his name struck me, even as an eleven-year-old. The Reverend wore a black suit and white shirt seven days a week. Winter, spring, summer, and fall, he always had on that suit. I once saw him cutting sugarcane in the dead of summer, and he was wearing that suit.

He was wearing it when he dunked me and my brothers in that filthy, tepid water, too. He wasn't in there with us, but he didn't even roll up his sleeves when he guided us one-by-one under the surface.

I emerged from the water expecting to see, smell, look, and be different, but nothing happened. Aside from a few claps and a "hab mercy" or two from Fat, the only thing baptizing got me was wet.

But when my eyes met my mama's, she was smiling.

I wanted to do it again.

*　*　*

Mama went to church every Sunday. She worshipped when she was there, and she seemed to receive true rest during those few hours every week. But she was also a true believer in black magic and the spirit world. A man named Gene Sallie lived about a quarter mile from us, and he was a "good witch doctor," a shaman, according to Mama. Mr. Sallie was a serious, but happy old man. He had no more than three teeth in his head, but he let you see them every time you'd come 'round.

"Come he-ya, chile," he'd smile. "Let me look atchoo … You are a good bow-ee." His accent let me know he wasn't from Sardis, but I never asked him. I assumed he came from what Mama referred to as the motherland.

I didn't know what that meant, either.

I liked to walk, so Mama would send me to meet Mr. Sallie every now and then to pick up her magic dust. In African culture, various salts are used to keep evil spirits and negative energy away. Mama believed in this practice with her whole heart. Mr. Sallie would send me back with rock salt; tiny stalactites—like the things that hang down from caves; pink chucks of salt; bags of salt powder; and even black salt—each having its own specific power to protect us from evil.

I never thought much about this. Mama would sprinkle salt in every room, around the yard, and along the road outside our home—consecrating our spaces, declaring them sacred and free from the darkness that defined Sardis.

Darkness like Uncle Kidd.

He was Fat's brother and as far as I ever knew, he lived with the *Hanks* and evil spirits in the wide-open spaces around the rest of us. I never saw his house. I only saw him standing on corners where one dirt road met another, or I'd see him from a distance, standing alone in a field talking to himself.

Mama never talked about Uncle Kidd other than to tell us to stay away from him. "That there's the evilest man to walk the earth," she'd whisper as we crossed to the other side of the road, or go inside the house should he appear nearby. According to my brothers and sisters, Uncle Kidd would put spells on people just to watch them suffer. If he didn't like the way you looked, or, heaven forbid you owed him money or the repayment of a favor, he could make a man's tongue swell up and choke him to death, or afflict someone with rashes, boils, or the fever.

When he died, Mama said that God gave Kidd everything he ever dealt, and killed him—painful and slow. I've always thought maybe Mr. Sallie had something to do with that. Just sitting back on his porch, quiet and smiling.

Those three teeth shining big and bright in the sun.

* * *

I never understood the idea of a God. I certainly had no personal image of Him. People would talk about God, and I would react about as I would if they mentioned the stars in the sky, or the wind.

I assumed He was a white man, because those were the only images I had ever seen. There was a picture of a praying Jesus behind the cash register at the market where I would go to get milk and rice and bread for Mama, and He had white skin, blue eyes, long, light-brown hair, and a beard that had obviously been shaped and trimmed by a professional.

He looked very *clean*.

So, I thought, God is another rich, light-skinned, white man. He is bigger than me, better than me, and He certainly doesn't live anywhere near Sardis.

My identity, all that I knew of myself, was in my skinny-scrawny-weak-as-water-poor-as-dirt-black-as-night-stuttering-stammering body. A fatherless, friendless fool.

I still wet my pants, for goodness' sake!

Mama would spank me when I wet my pants, and if I boo-booed, it was even worse. I didn't wet the bed, and I would never have an accident if I was alone. But I would urinate and defecate on myself when I was near Mama. Even as a ten-year-old. She would get so angry. I had younger siblings by this time, and even they didn't pee on themselves. I never had a good explanation for this. I don't think it was intentional, but maybe I liked the attention, painful as it was.

"How you ever gon' get out these woods if you can't control yo'self!" she'd scream as she held me up off of the ground by my wrist with one hand, and slap my backside wildly with the other.

"How you ever gon' get out that school?"

I actually enjoyed school. It was never a guarantee that I would make it there each morning, but it wasn't a chore for me like it was for my siblings. Shiloh School is a one-level, white brick building with six or eight classrooms, a lunchroom, and a makeshift library that doubled as a holding room before and after school where we'd wait and hope for a bus to show up and carry us home. Each classroom had a chalkboard, a bookshelf, cardboard cut-out letters and numbers stuck to the walls, and approximately ten to twelve desks—the kind that are all one piece, with the desk and chair connected, a basket underneath for books and papers and whatnot.

It took about an hour to walk from Cade Collins to the school, and that was a trek I would gladly make Monday through Friday if the weather would allow. I loved being in that tiny classroom. I felt *community* there. My stuttering was bad at this time, but not when I was reading. As slow and "unfortunate" as I was, I could read and write before I even went to school. Toni made sure of that before she left home for the Job Corps.

In those days, if a young person wanted out of poverty, especially out of a place like Sardis, they would enter the Job Corps and be assigned places to work, more often than not, close to home, but not Toni. I don't remember exactly when she left home, but one day she just wasn't there anymore. Other siblings would follow her to places unknown, leaving just six of us at Cade Collins.

All I knew was that the Promised Land was out there, and they must've found it.

I loved books. Even though I could read, I reveled in looking at the pictures of different people and places that didn't seem real. All I ever knew was right in front of me. Surely the ocean and the mountains and kings and queens were make-believe!

Most of the books at school were hand-me-down textbooks and manuals from the white schools, and they were always in rough shape—pages torn out, complete chapters removed or destroyed by scribbles, drawn pictures, or words scratched out by the original owners. The first time I ever saw the word "nigger," it was written in bold, green magic marker in the back of my Alabama history book, published in 1954.

The first time I was ever *called* a nigger was during the summer of my tenth year. We had just moved to Cade Collins House, and I was, of course, exploring the new-to-me fields and woods close by. It was as hot as it had ever been in my life. I remember seeing the sun's refraction even above the dried husks of corn on the ground ahead as I shuffled toward the woods to find shade. There was a small pond, about thirty feet across, near a short stretch of trees, and even though I couldn't yet swim, I made a beeline toward it and ran headlong into the waters. I can still feel the relief as I sank to the bottom and shot back up. The waters were only a few feet deep at the pond's center.

Standing there, I heard the faint screams of a man coming down the hill toward me. It was a white man riding a horse, and he was galloping toward me, screaming: "You stupid nigger! Get out of there, you dumb nigger! You're gonna die, nigger!" As he got closer, he was waving his arms, and then, "There's snakes in there, nigger! You're gonna get killed!"

Snakes?! I don't think my feet touched the ground as I scrambled out of that pond. In fact, that might be how I learned to swim. I splashed my way out just as the man on the horse made his way to me and "whoa'd" his horse to a halt.

"Are you okay?" His voice sounded like tires on a gravel road. "Answer me, boy? Are you bit?"

"N-n-n-n-naw, naw, naw suh," I stuttered.

"Well, that's a damn miracle," he huffed. "Get up outta here, now, and don't you come back," he shooed me away. "Are you kin to Fat?" he asked.

I was still struggling to catch my breath.

"Yeh-yeh-yeh, suh."

"Thought so," he said as he pulled the reins around the horse's head and headed back up the hill.

"Go on, now …" he called back.

And then he rode off—up the hill and out of sight. That's the last time I ever saw that man. It's funny though. The first time I ever got called a nigger probably saved my life. I was never scared of white people. I never thought about them very much. I feared them, but not because I thought they would hurt me. I just knew they were different. I knew they were superior. And I knew to stay away. I felt about them the way I probably would have felt about elephants if I had grown up in the Sahara. I know they exist. I've even seen a few. But I never really put myself in a situation to get trampled by any of them.

* * *

Mama Fat knew just about everybody in Sardis. Even the white people. After my family moved to Cade Collins, Fat actually moved in with a white man. She stayed with him until the day she died. He was the overseer to most of the land that surrounded us. A different family owned the land, but Jimmy—I forget his last name—was in charge of the day-in-day-out and used Fat as a live-in maid, cook, and whatever else his flesh desired.

Rumor had it that Jimmy and Fat stayed in the same room, but that she had to sleep on the floor at the foot of the bed after they would have relations.

It wouldn't be right for a white man and a Black woman to sleep in the same bed.

Everybody knew what was going on at Jimmy's, but no one ever said a word about it. Jimmy would have probably shot a man dead if he ever said anything woeful about Fat, and he would have shot him twice if they ever mentioned the sex.

That's just the way it was.

* * *

My interactions with white people would increase significantly a few weeks before I turned eleven years old. My two oldest brothers, Ronald and Donald, were starting to run around town more and more. They would spend time in Selma doing Lord knows what and only occasionally spend the night at Cade Collins. That was fine by the rest of us, because it would mean we'd only have to sleep three to a mattress, and back then, that was quite the luxury.

One night, or perhaps in the early hours of the morning, I awoke to the glare of a flashlight in my face and the cries of Mama and my little brothers, who had been sleeping on the first of three mattresses in a row on the floor. Me, Andre, and Vernon were sprawled out on the second.

"That's not him!" she was screaming. "That's Alton! That's just Alton!"

I was squinting and holding my arms in front of my face trying to block the glare, when I noticed three shotguns pointed at me and my brothers. Vernon, who was probably eight or nine at the time, scrambled to the corner of the mattress, against the wall, and pulled his knees impossibly close to his chest. He was terrified, crying, and sucking his thumb. Andre, who had been sleeping in the middle, between us, instinctively pulled me backward and positioned himself between me and the men waving their barrels. Holding his hand up to shield us from the bullets that never came.

"They ain't here, Sheriff!" Mama was pleading with the men. "These is good boys! These ain't them!"

The sheriff and three of his men—out-of-uniform deputies, or civilians, we can't be sure—were looking for Ronald and Donald.

It seems my two older brothers had quite a side business going. For the past few weeks, those particular Hardy boys had been letting themselves into the intermediate school a few miles away by way of a broken window near the back roofline. Once inside, they helped themselves to large bags of cereal, pallets of milk cartons, potato chips, candy, crates of Pepsi, and ohmygoodness, maybe God *is* real … honey buns.

They had been stealing the food for a couple of weeks and hiding their haul in the cornfield next to Cade Collins. Once the rest of us kids found this out, we encouraged them to continue their plundering, because, did I mention the honey buns?

"Where are they, Belle?" One of the men swung his barrel around and pointed it at Mama.

"I don't know, sir. We ain't seen 'em since night 'fo last." She pleaded with him, "Nobody here knows where they are."

He lowered his gun.

"We're going to find them, Belle. And when we do, there ain't nothing gonna save them. You tell them to turn themselves in, or we're gonna handle it ourselves …"

And then they left, quicker than they showed up.

I hadn't seen my brothers in a couple of days. None of us knew where they spent their time away from the house. I assumed they went to my father's in Selma, but surely the sheriff looked for them there. Mama closed the door and collapsed behind it, weeping and moaning.

Not one of us went back to sleep that night.

A few days later, I was walking home from school when I saw chaos unfolding at Cade Collins. The sheriff and four men this time were pulling Andre from the house. Mama was crying, "He's not them! He's not them!" I can't recall who all was there at the time, but I can still see the fear in Andre's eyes as they met mine and a noose was put around his neck.

The next few minutes play back as if in slow motion. Mama was on her knees, screaming. Andre was stood up on the back of a pickup truck, and the rope connected to his thirteen-year-old body was thrown up and over the tree limb that extended into our front yard.

I remember Vernon, expressionless on the front porch, sucking his thumb. Two of the men readied themselves with the straight end of the rope and one of them whistled: two short blasts.

The truck edged forward and Andre scrambled to find structure with his toes. He hung there for five seconds, looking like a catfish thrashing at the end of a line. Five seconds:

Thousand one.
Thousand two.
Thousand three.
Thousand four.
Thousand fi…

The truck moved back into place and Andre found footing in its bed. He was crying and supporting the weight of his body by clinging to the twine.

I ran to Mama and screamed for her to make them stop. "Please, Mama! Make them go away!"

"Where are they, nigger? Where are those boys?" One of the men yelled toward Mama and then whistled again. The truck moved forward. Andre kicked and flailed. Tears were streaming down his cheeks and his eyes looked like they would explode at any second. He was trying to scream, but his voice wouldn't come. He just coughed and groaned. Thousand one. Thousand two. Thousand three. Thousand four … The man whistled again, and the truck's tires spun as the driver sped forward.

Thousand five.
Thousand six.
Thousand seven.

Another whistle.

The two men released their grip on the rope, and Andre came crashing down in a heap at their feet. Mama and I rushed to him, but he was already crawling, scrambling to the porch. Still coughing, eyes still streaming tears.

"We're gonna find those boys, Belle. And if we don't, we'll just come back for the rest of you. Do you understand me?"

Mama couldn't even bring herself to meet his eyes. She sat there in a pile in our front yard, crying to herself as they loaded up and drove away.

Three days later, we would leave Sardis for good.

*   *   *

It was a Saturday morning. I remember that it was cool outside. Strangely cool. I was on the front porch—throating out exhales in quick puffs to see if the air would freeze—when Andre came running out and yelled, "He's here!" Our brother, Eddie, came tearing up the dirt road in a small U-Haul truck driving way too fast. He skidded to a stop in the grass about three feet from the front door, smiled, and said, "Time a' go."

I didn't know where we were going, only what Mama had told us the night before. She handed each of us a black dobbage tag—which is what I thought garbage bags were called my entire life—and told us to put our favorite things in them. "We're going on an adventure 'morrow mornin'," she said. "Shorts, shirts, pants, draws, and shoes. That's it. Ain't no need for nothin' else where we goin'."

I hardly slept that night. *An adventure?* I could hardly process the word, much less the idea of what she had in mind. My life to that point had been a lonely journey—a quiet stroll through the woods and fields of home. Adventures only existed in books and stories told by old people and folks who weren't from Sardis.

What did she mean, "Ain't no need for nothin' else where we goin'"?

Ten minutes after Eddie showed up, Cade Collins dissolved in the truck's rearview, and I had the feeling that my life was about to begin.

I wasn't being taken from Sardis, Alabama; I was being delivered.

Half-full dobbage tag in tow.

NOT MY HOME

June 1977

*   *   *

I couldn't contain myself in the truck. I was insufferable. My excitement level was soaring, which accentuated my stutter and led to unending questions:

"Wh-wh-wh-what's tha-a-a-a-t? W-w-w-w-here i-i-i-is th-th-this road t-t-t-taking taking taking us? L-l-l-l-ook, Mama! L-l-l-ook at the tuh-tuh-tuh-trucks. Ca-a-a-a-a-an w-w-w-we ssssstop a-a-a-again? How-how-how fffffarrrr is Lou-lou-lou-lllllllouisville?"

450 miles.

That's how far Louisville, Kentucky, is from Sardis, Alabama. A full day's drive. A world away. And I didn't shut up for a single inch of it.

To look at a map, the drive is simple and straightforward—a perfect line can be drawn from Selma through Birmingham, Huntsville, Nashville, Bowling Green, and Elizabethtown.

But there was nothing simple or straightforward about this pilgrimage. To me, it was magic. In all of my eleven years, I had never seen anything like what lay before us on that trip.

Every field was a new world to be discovered. Every tree, a new creation. Every fence post, telephone pole, billboard, speed limit or directional sign, and car after car after truck after trailer that we passed was a brand-new experience.

Just before Nashville, we found ourselves in a traffic jam, and, while it frustrated Eddie, I was fascinated. *A traffic jam?* No. It was the single most remarkable event of my life. Seemingly thousands of vehicles full of seemingly millions of people were slowly inching north. Together.

I had never seen an Asian person before, so I was mesmerized by the family that pulled up next to us: a man, a woman, a boy about my age, a young girl, and a baby. They looked like dolls. Their faces were happy, round, and decidedly different from the ones I was used to. The little girl saw me staring down at them from the truck and smiled. I jerked my head away, embarrassed, but then looked back as she and her brother were contorting their faces and laughing. The boy took his pointer finger and placed it to his nose, pushing the end of it up like a pig's snout. The girl used both of her pointer fingers to pull on either side of her mouth as she stuck out and wagged her tongue.

They continued to laugh as their car pulled ahead, and they waved goodbye as their father changed lanes and began inching up the exit ramp and out of sight. As ridiculous as it may seem, I felt like the three of us made a connection in those few minutes together on Interstate 65, and I felt an immediate sadness when I realized that I would never see their silly faces again.

I wasn't used to that type of connection—unexpected joy—and felt I would never smile like that again. I slinked back in the seat and quietly hoped that this traffic jam would never end.

* * *

Newburg, Kentucky, is a small, predominately Black neighborhood within the Louisville city limits where my brother Eddie had been living for the past few months. After word got to him about what the police had done to Andre, he rented the U-Haul with all the money he had and planned his roundtrip journey to save his family—at least the six of us who were still lost in Sardis. We arrived at a tiny, two-bedroom house well past midnight, and I fell fast asleep on the floor next to Mama. When daylight hit the curtainless windows of the den, I woke up ready to explore my new home.

Stepping over the sleeping bodies of my brothers and sisters, I ventured into a short hallway that led to a closet-sized bathroom with a toilet, sink, and stand-up shower. I had never seen these things in a house before. Running water was a luxury known only to white folks and people who lived in the brick houses near Selma. We had certainly never had the opportunity to flush our own toilet or wash ourselves in a shower controlled by knobs labeled "hot" and "cold."

I was in awe. Next to the bathroom was a bedroom where Eddie and three others were sleeping. One of them—a girl I didn't recognize—turned toward me and smiled before immediately falling back asleep. In the kitchen, there was a table and two chairs, a sink, a stove, an oven, and a refrigerator about half the size of the ones I had seen in the food stores back home.

The walls of the house were solid, strong, and painted white. One of the bedrooms had wallpaper with printed flowers and palm branches. I was mesmerized by that wallpaper. I could have spent all day exploring the patterns and petals—how the white flowers always grew next to the red; the way the palm fronds spread victoriously out over the oranges, pinks, and blues. I thought I could see a bird and a butterfly, too. It was beautiful.

I counted eleven people, total, in the house that morning. Most of them were family, but several others were simply staying there for a while, and would come in and out over the coming weeks and months as we settled in to Newburg.

Most days, Mama would wake up and leave before the sun or the rest of us were awake, and she'd stay gone until long after dark. I never asked her where she went during the day. Nobody talked much about anything in that house. I assumed she was cleaning homes and offices in Edgewood, Lynnview, or all the way up in Watterson Park, where a lot of white people lived. "Maid" was a common job for women from my neighborhood, and Mama sure knew how to keep a clean space. After a few days marveling at my new home—with wall-to-wall carpet, lights in the ceilings, a toilet that flushed *almost* every time, and windows that looked out into a chain-link-fenced yard—I picked up where I left off in Sardis and started walking around.

I saw a sign one day that read:

"Newburg was settled in the 1830s by four German immigrant families… Newburg is a German word that means New Town."

I'll say.

Newburg was all so remarkably new, yet somehow familiar. The gravel roads, dirt paths, and cotton fields of Alabama had simply been replaced with black asphalt, sidewalks, and parking lots, and my days were still a common collection of lonely hours, walking by myself.

Newburg Middle School rests a bit uncomfortably and somewhat out of place among the crackerbox ranch houses of the neighborhood where we lived. It's a big, red brick building that sits at the end of Exeter Avenue—a flat and straight-as-an-arrow street with sidewalks on both sides.

Our house on Rosette Boulevard was about a mile and a half from the school, but only a quarter of a mile through the overgrown yards and ramshackle fences that separated property lines and attempted to restrict dogs from roaming the streets. That was my preferred route, actually. To me, the bus was a much scarier prospect than the potential of being yelled at by neighbors or chased down by a Rottweiler while trespassing.

There were people on the bus.

People I didn't know.

Even white people.

My first day at Newburg Middle School was my first day of seventh grade. I was terrified as I entered the large, white doors that led into the expansive welcome area.

Am I dressed right?
How will I know where to go?
What if I'm in the wrong place?
Will I understand how they talk?
Will they understand me?
Will they even see me?

I had to pee.

Mrs. Harper's eyes met mine as soon as I stepped inside. As she made her way through the sea of children—all seemingly comfortable in this massive place, all happily greeting one another after a long summer vacation—I looked frantically for a direction in which to run.

To escape.

Mrs. Harper was a big woman, like Mama, but even taller. Her jet-black hair rested, hard as a rock, atop her gigantic head, and her bright red fingernails—a foot long if they were an inch—reflected the sun that shined through the skylight above, making it seem like she was approaching me with ten bloody swords.

My bottom lip quivered, but then, with a slight knowing tilt of her enormous head, she smiled … As if she had once been in my shoes, worn out and ragged as they were. As if she, too, had been forced to endure being different, feeling lost and alone. Maybe she didn't look the same as other people; maybe she didn't dress right, talk right, or know where the hell the bathroom was.

Her smile was the most beautiful and genuine thing I'd ever seen. She floated over to me and knelt down. Suddenly, my fear turned to a feeling of acceptance, and I began to weep. My arms fell limp to my sides and I stood there, crying, resting in the arms of an angel. She took me to the boys restroom, cleared the place of a few eighth graders who were lingering before class, and cleaned me up.

"My name's Mrs. Harper," she said, kindly. "You must be Alton Hardy."

"Y-y-y-y-esssss m-m-m …" I struggled to make sound. "It's okay, son. Everything 'gon be alright." She put her hand to my face and smiled again. "Let's get you to class, shall we?"

We entered room 119 together. She held my trembling hand in hers and guided me to a third-row seat between a beautiful girl named Mary and a kid named Marvin, who was chewing on the collar of his shirt.

"'Sup?" Marvin nodded.

I nodded back.

The rest of the day is a blur, and I can't truly recall much more from my first few months at Newburg. But I'll never forget Mrs. Harper and the love she showed me that day. It wouldn't be long before Newburg started to feel like home. Whatever that means.

* * *

I'll also never forget the social workers. Every month, a government worker—usually a tall, skinny, white woman with legs as long as flagpoles—would come to visit the house, "just to make sure y'all are livin' right," she'd say. She would come in smiling, and almost always leave in a fit. More than likely, one of my brothers was causing a commotion, trying to distract her from pulling the cushions off the couch, undressing our beds, and rummaging through our closets. She was looking for a man.

She was looking for my father.

Back then, and probably still today, government welfare checks were dependent on your situation. Mama claimed there was no man in the house, so she got a few more dollars every month. If Mrs. Flagpole Legs had found my father living with us, the checks would have stopped altogether.

"Having a man ain't worth it, no way," Mama said.

She was constantly trying to figure out a way to move us—me, Toni, Andre, Vernon, Charles, and Niles—to a bigger house. There were too many people and not enough sections of floor to sleep on. I loved it at Rosette, and the thought of leaving scared me to death. I didn't want to lose what little feeling of community we had been able to establish there.

But Mama was determined, and once that woman put her mind to something, it was as good as done.

I cried the day we moved to Portier Street. The new house was almost identical to Rosette—right down to the tiny refrigerator and the orange and brown speckled carpet in the front room and hallway—but moving was change. And I was tired and terrified of change.

I woke up on a Sunday morning to voices outside the front room window. We called it a front room and not a den, because dens have couches and chairs and coffee tables. Our front room had two mattresses and a laundry basket full of photo albums and important documents, such as my brand-new immunization form.

I hadn't ever been to a pediatrician in Sardis. Once Newburg Middle School learned this, they sent me to get tested for everything under the sun. Mama took me to the health clinic where the doctors and nurses treated me like a science project—they gathered around me as if I were a creature from another planet and then proceeded to poke, prod, stick, grab, and look at places on my body I had never even seen myself.

Over the next six weeks, I had to go back multiple times to make sure all of my immunizations and boosters and blood work were up to date. Those folks got twelve years of examinations done in a month and a half.

I pushed the laundry basket over next to the window and sat in it while watching four kids—all around my age—bounce a basketball back and forth outside on the street. One of the boys was familiar. It was Marvin, from Mrs. Harper's class! He recognized me, too, and waved for me to come outside. I instinctively hid under the window and closed my eyes impossibly tight. Maybe if I was still, quiet, and made myself small enough, they wouldn't see me and I wouldn't have to explain why I was hiding, stalking their every move.

Suddenly, there was a knock at the door. And then another. And another. "Hey, boy!" I heard a voice call from outside. "You play ball?" He continued and knocked again.

I opened the door slowly and met Marvin's familiar smile.

"You just move in?" he asked.

I nodded.

"You play ball?"

I shrugged, slightly, and slinked a bit further behind the door. "We was about to play a game. You wanna come?"

I desperately wanted to say no, but I was even more desperate for a friend. I stepped out from behind the door and walked with Marvin to meet the others who waited at the edge of the cul-de-sac. "This here Anthony," he said, pointing to a short, husky kid who crossed his arms on his chest like he was posing for a portrait. "That one's 'Pooh,'" he motioned, and Pooh stuck out his chin.

"And that's Anthony's stepbrother, Lamont."

At that, the boy named Lamont, a light-skinned brother with a smile as big as his face, outstretched his hand and nodded for me to shake. I had never done that before. I'd seen others shake hands, give high-fives and hand-slaps, and even lean in to give an elbow-bump combined with a brief hug or slap on the back, but I had never done anything like that in my life.

Lamont took my hand and squeezed it. "Hey, man," he laughed. "You gotta squeeze back or else it's weird!" The others joined him, laughing, and I squeezed ever so slightly, then jerked my hand away as if it had just been stung by a bee.

"It's cool," he said, holding his hands up as if to say, "No offense," and continued, "we can work on that later. You wanna play ball or what?"

Lamont turned and called for Pooh to pass him the basketball. He then bounced it between his legs and called back over his shoulder: "Only my mama calls me Lamont," he said. "You can call me L.A."

From that moment on, Marvin, Anthony, L.A., and a boy named Pooh would become my first, best friends. The four of them accepted me into their group immediately. I became a sort of project for them to work on together. I still had a stutter, I was painfully shy, I had no confidence in anything I ever tried to do, and I had nothing at all to offer them. They just liked me for some reason. And I loved them with my whole heart.

L.A. was the definition of cool. He was two years older than the rest of us, but it wasn't his age that made him special. He was tall, muscular, athletic, light-skinned, and popular with boys *and* girls.

And he was always smiling.

He just had a way about him that made others want to follow his lead.

We didn't have a basketball hoop, but that didn't stop us from playing ball every day. L.A. created a game we called curb-ball.

Here's how it worked:

It was every man for himself. The player with the ball would dribble and try to get past the others without getting the ball stolen. To score points, the player would try to shoot the ball toward the curb and hit the edge just right so that it would catapult back into the cul-de-sac and land within different squares we had drawn on the cement with a rock, or a piece of chalk. Each square had a different point value, and the first player to 20, or 50, or sometimes even 200, would be the winner. We played curb-ball for hours and hours after school and on weekends.

No one ever beat L.A.

This was the happiest time in my life. I not only had a close group of friends, but others began to accept me, too—mostly because I was in the group with L.A., but even as I stuttered my way through seventh and eighth grade, I was beginning to have an identity. I was still very quiet and hardly spoke unless I was spoken to. My friends started calling me "Cool Breeze," because I was so quiet.

L.A. was constantly trying to break me out of my shell. He'd punch me in the shoulder or sometimes trip me or push me down to try and get a reaction. We'd all laugh it off, and I'd end up stammering my way through a string of curse words, or make a joke that if he'd shut up every once in a while, "m-m-m-maybe I could g-g-g-g-get a wor-r-r-r-rd out."

Other times, he'd just give me a look, or put his hand on my shoulder and say something like, "It's all good, Cool Breeze. I know you got a voice in that big head of yours. I just wish you would use it every now and then."

There was a girl on our street named Cheryl Graves whom we all dreamed about. She was a year older than me—a year younger than L.A.—and she knew we all had girl-next-door fantasies about her. We were all pretty sure that L.A. had tangible experience to fuel most of *his* fantasies, but neither he nor Cheryl ever owned up to it. In fact, she spent most of her time flirting with the quiet kid from Sardis, which never made sense, but every time she'd bat an eyelash or give a "Heeeeeey, Altoooooooon!" from across the street, the entire cul-de-sac would erupt in laughter, and my black face would turn a bright pink. Every time.

When we weren't playing curb-ball or making fun of each other out in the neighborhood, the five of us would make our way to Bashford Manor Mall. I would walk. They would ride bikes. I couldn't afford a bicycle, and even if I could, I had never learned to ride. Pooh and Marvin tried to teach me a few times, but that always ended with my knees and elbows bleeding, or another story they could put in their *Cool Breeze Is an Idiot* file to bring out and embarrass me with later—usually in front of Cheryl.

At the mall, we'd hang out in the parking lot or try to finagle leftovers from classmates and other friends who might be enjoying a meal at the food court. All of us were poor, but just like everything else, there are levels to poverty, and I was at the very bottom.

In Sardis, there was no such thing as social class. There were just Black folks and white folks. It wasn't until I moved away from Alabama that "haves and have-nots" became a reality. Some say there are four social classes: Upper, Middle, Working Class, and Lower. Others break it down even more: Upper, Upper Middle, Middle, Working, and Lower. I've even heard of a deeper take on the classes that includes Higher Upper Class and Lower Lower Class.

At the end of the day, classifications don't matter that much. All I know is I might have had a pot to pee in, but it was almost always broken and we couldn't afford to get it fixed.

I wore the same clothes almost every day. My friends noticed this about me but never made a thing of it. From time to time, Anthony, who seemed to grow a size bigger every week, would give me an old T-shirt or a pair of shorts that he had outgrown, but most of what I had were hand-me-downs from my brothers—all of which were stained, damaged, or ill-fitting to the point that I'd rather just stay in the same pants and shirt Monday through Friday.

Sometimes, my four friends would go to the skating rink nearby and then to White Castle or Burger King on Thursday nights. I never did that. It only cost $2 to skate back then, but $2 might as well have been $200 to me. When you have nothing, even a little bit is too much.

It wasn't all bad. Being the poor kid among poor kids was a struggle, but I think not having any money saved me from a lot of embarrassment at times. First of all, I couldn't skate. But also, this was 1979. Disco music was giving way to the birth of hip-hop, and songs like "Rapper's Delight" by the Sugar Hill Gang were on every radio station, 8-track deck, stereo, and playing loudly in skating rinks throughout the country:

> *I said-a hip, hop, the hippie, the hippie*
> *To the hip hip hop-a you don't stop the rock*
> *It to the bang-bang boogie, say up jump the boogie*
> *To the rhythm of the boogie, the beat …*

This was my nightmare. I was a stutterer. It would take me half an hour just to get out the first line of that song, much less rap along with it. They could have their fun with the skates and the sodas and the hamburgers and the girls and the impossible-to-sing hip-hop.

I was just fine reading, doing homework, or exploring the city alone.

* * *

I don't recall ever feeling sadness when I lived in Sardis. Sure, I was lonely, alone, lost, and on the path to nowhere, but I didn't know any better. So sadness never crept in.

But I got *sad* in Newburg.

I had community, relationships, and all that I had longed for from the people around me, but Newburg was also an awakening. When you sleepwalk through life, you experience things, but you don't necessarily feel them. I experienced life in Sardis, but I was almost fifteen years old before I ever felt the sting of being aware.

> *I didn't have money.*
> *I didn't have the right clothes.*
> *I didn't have the right words.*
> *I didn't have a bicycle.*
> *And I didn't have a father.*

Even among friends—true friends who saw me, knew me, and loved me no matter what—I was alone. I was different. I was … less than. And I was *still* searching and hoping for something I could not see.

Anthony's dad—L.A.'s stepdad—was a man named Bobby Carr. He was young, good-looking, fun, funny, and deeply involved in his sons' lives. He would wrestle them in their front yard, they'd listen to music together, tell jokes to each other, spend time working on projects around their house, and he would even play curb-ball with us from time to time.

On weekends, he would pay me and L.A. to wash his car—a spotless, white, 1976 Camaro—and then let L.A. drive to White Castle where we would spend our dollar-fifty on milkshakes or French fries or Pepsis.

Bobby Carr was the first example of a loving father that I had ever seen. He played that role for a lot of us. Pooh and Marvin didn't have fathers in their homes, either. Not many of our friends or classmates did. Not the Black kids, anyway.

I imagined all white families were like the Carrs, but with money. They were probably all in the Upper or Higher Upper or whatever class says, "All of our dads love us and still live at home."

My second year at Newburg Middle School was the first time I ever really interacted with white people—especially white people my age. It was 1980, and somebody somewhere thought it was about time to not just theoretically integrate the schools in Louisville, but to actually put salt and pepper in the same shaker.

It did not go well.

Five years earlier, Newburg made national news as riots broke out throughout the entire county. It seems folks were less than pleased when, in order to promote equality, the courts ordered that Blacks were to be bused to all white schools on the other side of the county and vice versa.

The "bus riots" completely upended Newburg, and the violence caused a state of emergency as bottles and rocks and even Molotov Cocktails were hurled at some of the buses carrying Blacks from the West End to predominantly white neighborhoods uptown.

When I was at Newburg, there weren't a lot of riots to speak of, but there were a lot of fights. White families were still unsettled that their children had to be bused to "those places," and they let us know pretty quickly how they felt—especially if we ever found ourselves within spitting distance.

I was walking alone from school to my house one afternoon when I heard a whistle burst, followed by a high-pitched "Hey, boy!"

A green Buick pulled next to me and slowed to a stop. I glanced at the car but kept walking.

"Hey, boy! I'm talking to you! You stupid or something?"

There were two men in the car. They looked to be in their early twenties—probably college students—but shadows sketched across their faces and I couldn't see.

"Do I know you, sir?" I asked and leaned closer to the open window. As my eyes lowered to meet his, the passenger cast a vicious stream of sputum from his mouth that covered the entire left side of my face.

"No. You don't know me, nigger. And you never will."

He sounded both calm and pleased with himself when he turned to the driver and smiled. "We can go now."

I coughed and gagged and quickly pulled off my shirt to wipe the spit from my eye and mouth. I wasn't mad. I wasn't sad. I was in shock. I didn't even blink as I shuffled the last quarter of a mile home. I couldn't believe what had just happened, and I didn't say a word about it to anyone, because *surely* they would never believe this could happen. I never would have.

That wasn't even the last time I would be the target of such personalized hate that year. Whether it was on the way to or from school, in the classroom, cafeteria, library, or gym, the white people in my life never failed to let me and my friends know that they didn't belong in the same space as us; and if they had to be there, we certainly didn't belong with them.

* * *

The next year, my freshman year of high school, the county decided to officially close Thomas Jefferson High School in Newburg, which meant that I had to make a twenty-five-minute bus ride to Moore High School in Louisville. It was a white school in a beautiful neighborhood with manicured lawns, big, clean, beautiful houses, and driveways full of cars.

It looked perfect on the outside. Inside, the natives were restless. Fights happened every day. Some were worse than others, but they always ended with a group of white kids tormenting or torturing a Black kid. Never the other way around. Strength in numbers is a powerful truth, and the Blacks were not many—not nearly enough—at Moore High School.

* * *

I started to hate school. What used to be a place for community was now another daily reminder that I was not where I was supposed to be. It was a place of loneliness and dread.

L.A. did fine at school. He was somehow beloved no matter where he was—in the neighborhood and even at white school.

Maybe it was his light skin. Maybe it was because he was such a great athlete. But his experience was not shared by me and my other brothers from Newburg. I was still searching for my place. I was still desperate for belonging.

Mama started going to church at the tiny Church of Christ just down the street from our house. I don't know how she got there the first time, and I'm not sure how she convinced me to go—I probably didn't have a choice—but I began attending every *church day* during my freshman year in school.

At first, I just went for the doughnuts.

Every Sunday morning, a white, twelve-passenger Econoline van with "Newburg Church of Christ" emblazoned on its side would pull up at the edge of our neighborhood and welcome any and all residents to climb aboard and be taken to Newburg's version of Shangri-La: *a basement level fellowship hall filled with all the doughnuts you could eat.*

It was glorious. My friends didn't understand my excitement for Sunday mornings, but to be fair, most of their cupboards were full. I still lived with six other people, and even when there was food in the house, very few crumbs found their way down the pecking order to me.

When you're a hungry, inner-city kid, you're gonna go where the food is—especially if there's sugar involved.

Some Saturday nights I would find it difficult to fall asleep just thinking about the manna from heaven that awaited me the next morning.

One particular church day, after I was all filled up with God's blessings of sugar-sprinkled dough, I went to the church service, alone. The sounds coming from the tiny sanctuary lured me in— the combined voices of worshippers:

Soon and very soon, we are going to see the King.
Soon and very soon, we are going to see the King.
Soon and very soon, we are going to see the King …

And this is what got me:

Alleluia. Alleluia. We are going to see the King.

There was something in the way the congregation and choir came together on "Alleluia!" that gave me chills and made me want to be in that moment. To stay in that moment. To jump up and sing with them. To be a part of what they were singing and believing and feeling as much as possible.

So I kept going.

Sometimes, I'd pass by L.A. and others on my way to worship and they would seize the opportunity to poke fun or call me crazy, but I loved going. I found community there. I started learning the books of the Bible—and not just because the teachers promised more doughnuts, cookies, or chocolate milk to those of us who could recite Scripture or name the prophets in alphabetical order. That certainly helped, but it was more than that for me. I loved learning and hearing what the leaders of that tiny church had to say.

I even started going on my own. Mama would go sometimes, and my brothers would join me from time to time—for the doughnuts—but I was there every chance I got: Wednesday nights, Sunday mornings, Sunday nights. Church days.

I began to be changed. I would get "happiness," which is what the elders called being moved by the Spirit. Now, whether the Holy Spirit was literally moving me to jump up, clap and raise my hands, and inadvertently holler "Alleluia!" during a particularly high-energy sermon, I don't know. Maybe I was just copying the older, more spiritually advanced and animated members of the church, but it was genuine to me. This feeling was true. This community was love. This God was real.

I was baptized on a Wednesday night. Standing in the baptismal pool with one of my pastors—*the Right Reverend so and so*—I felt a sense of peace come over me that I haven't the words to describe differently. It was a stillness and warmth. This was not at all like the outdoor trough I was pushed under in Sardis. This water was clean, and the reverend was gentle as he guided me under:

"And having been commissioned by our Lord and Savior, Jesus Christ, I baptize you, Alton Hardy—my brother—in the name of the Father, and of the Son, and of the Holy Spirit. Amen."

I could hear the roar of the congregation even while I was still under the water—the muffled sounds of jubilation grew louder and clearer as I was brought up and out, and I wept. Echoes from Mama's hope for me and my brothers years earlier rang in my head: *"Come Sunday mornin', y'all gone be different."*

Something happened to me that day. Something unexpected. Something beautiful. Something supernatural.

I *was* different.

* * *

One church day—it was February 20, my mama's birthday—I was headed to church alone. Before leaving, I peeked through the crack of Mama's bedroom door and saw her curled up in her bedsheets, holding her stomach, and weeping into her pillow.

She cried a lot in those days. Food was extremely scarce in our home. We had no heat. Our electricity would sometimes go out for days at a time until she or my brothers could make a few dollars and beg the power company for grace. It was hard on all of us, but especially her. She had nobody. She must have felt so alone.

At least in Sardis there were family members and people she knew close by: Mama Fat, brothers and sisters, even Mr. Sallie was always at the ready to sprinkle salts in hopes for better days. When it was cold back home, you could just build a fire. In Newburg, you just stayed cold.

Or, you went to church. The heat always worked at the church.

"Mama, you wanna go to church with me?"

She didn't answer.

"Come on, Mama, we can warm up. I think the choir's gone sing."

Nothing.

"You want me to stay home with you?"

"Go." She managed to form the word and waved for me to leave her alone.

On the way out, I quietly stepped over my little brothers, Vernon and Niles, still sleeping, but when I got to Andre, I shook him awake.

"Andre!" I whispered. "Andre, wake up." He opened his eyes and stared at me, blankly. "Today is Mama's birthday." I squatted down so that my face was close to his. "Today is Mama's birthday," I repeated.

"Whatchoo want me do, Alton? Bake her a cake?" He pushed me away and rolled back over to sleep.

He wasn't wrong. What did I expect him to do? We had no money. She had no friends. It's not like we could throw her a party or buy her a gift. Even if we could, what do you buy a person who has nothing?

Turtles!

As I walked to the end of our street to board the church van, it hit me that Mama's favorite thing in the whole world was chocolate covered pecans and caramel. They were called Turtles, and I had the distinct memory of watching her eat Turtle candies and laughing. I don't know where we were, what else she was doing, or how she got them, but in my memory, she was happy.

I need to get her some Turtles.

Instead of getting on the van that morning, I turned left down a side street and started walking toward the mall and praying out loud: "Jesus, if you are real, please help me get Mama them Turtles." I imagine now, someone sitting on his front porch, enjoying a cup of coffee, when a scrawny Black kid comes walking by, crying out in Jesus' name for Turtles. I'm sure I was a sight to behold.

This is the first time I remember praying so specifically, and it was definitely the first time I prayed out loud:

"Please, Jesus, I want to get these for Mama. Dear holy, magnificent, majestic, and wonderful Father," now I was really pouring it on, "Lord if you hear your children and know the truth in their hearts, hear me now: Lord, send me twenty dollars so I can buy Mama them Turtles."

Twenty dollars. I don't know why I asked for twenty dollars. Why not five or ten or, better yet, ten thousand? But I asked for twenty.

To get to the Bashford Manor Mall from where we lived, I'd have to walk on trails through the woods leading to the highway, where I could cross four lanes of traffic and then spill out into the parking lot of the apartments that had recently been built across the street and a few blocks down from the mall. As I got to the apartment complex, I was still praying:

"Twenty dollars, Lord. Please, God."

Out of the corner of my eye, I saw a group of white kids—all girls, younger than me, about five or six years old—playing ring around the rosy in the parking lot. They were all wearing dresses and probably waiting on their parents to take them to the Baptist church down the street. As I turned to watch them play, I looked down.

There was a twenty-dollar bill.

It was folded neatly in half and resting on the ground between two cars. A rush of heated adrenaline poured over my entire body as I leaned down to pick up the money. I quickly looked around to see if anyone was watching me—to see if the person who lost the money might be coming back for it. But no one was there. Just the little girls, who stopped their game for a few seconds and waved at me from across the lot.

I waved back and then took off running toward the mall. I was laughing and screaming and crying and praising God all at the same time.

"Look what you did, God!" I screamed. "Thank you, Jesus! Look what you just did!"

My feet hardly touched the ground as I ran home with Mama's extra-large box of candy, a birthday card, and the change left over from my purchase. When I got there, I signed the card, "Your son, Alton" and placed it and the candy outside of her bedroom door. Then, I sprinted as fast as I could to Newburg Church of Christ, where I happily put $9.62 in the offering plate.

That day, February 20, 1980, is when I began to believe that God is real, and He loves me. And that's the day I developed a thirst for seeing Him show up.

Later that afternoon, after I returned from church, Mama came out of her bedroom and pulled me to herself, squeezed, slightly, and then slapped the side of my head with her palm. "Boy, how dare you spend that kind of money on me! Don't you never do that nonsense again!" The sting of her hand was still ringing in my ears when she added, "But I sho' do love them Turtles." And she smiled.

* * *

I wasn't a perfect kid. Far from it. L.A., Anthony, Marvin, and Pooh were still the biggest influences in my life. I loved church day, but I lived for hanging out with my friends. As we got a little older, activities like curb ball were replaced by flirting with girls, smoking cigarettes, and experimenting with alcohol. Mostly, I would just take sips from L.A.'s bottle—he always had a bottle. I didn't much care for whiskey, but L.A. seemed to love the stuff.

He was having sex, too. Lots of it. Girls would flock to be by his side, and he leaned completely into his reputation as the smooth-talking, good-looking, cigarette-smoking, bourbon-drinking, light-skinned brother of Portier Street.

He was the coolest guy in the world.

Now, while L.A. and my other friends were growing up the fun way in the hood, I was forced to grow up the hard way. I had to get a job. President Carter had recently reinstated the Comprehensive Employment and Training Act, which was a program that trained workers and provided jobs in public service, predominantly summer jobs for inner city kids over the age of fifteen. None of my friends worked at the time, but I got employed at Newburg Public Park. It was a pretty, but also pretty run-down area with a small, open field, swing sets and a jungle gym, and picnic tables that doubled as platforms to have sex on and make drug deals at after the sun went down.

Each morning, I would walk around the park with a dobbage tag and clean up the remnants of the previous night's debauchery—cigarette butts, pill boxes, hypodermic needles, beer cans and liquor bottles, and condoms. Hopefully before kids and families made their way to enjoy the day.

I got paid $400 to work the park that summer, and suddenly I felt like the richest kid in Kentucky. I had never seen so much money. My father worked the cotton and corn fields in Sardis for more than twelve years and got paid in rotten apples and corn cobs. Mama worked every single day making white people's houses sparkle and shine, and she got paid a fraction of what I made just by scooping up the trash that my friends would leave behind after a night of play in our proverbial backyard.

It was electrifying. I had money for the first time in my life, and I could do anything I wanted with it. I could buy new clothes. I could pay the rent. I could pay the electric, water, or gas bill. I could buy Mama a proper sofa or coffee table for the front room.

Or I could buy a bike. I had learned to ride a few weeks earlier, and I knew exactly what I wanted.

A bright, white Schwinn bicycle with a red, cushioned seat and knobby tires … spokes shiny as the sun.

I'll never forget riding that bike over to L.A.'s and Anthony's house for the first time. The two of them came running out to meet me, squealing like little girls. Not only were they impressed with the beauty of "White Lightning," but they were genuinely happy for me. It had been a long two years walking beside them or sitting on the handlebars of whichever one of them drew the short straw.

Now, I was equal.

That's the first and only thing that I had ever owned—the only thing that was mine and mine alone. Every pair of shoes had been a hand-me-down or thrift-store find. Every shirt, pair of pants, shorts, and even underwear had always belonged to someone else first.

White Lightning was mine.

I washed it after every ride. I rolled it inside my house at the end of each day and slept beside it in our bedroom. I was so proud, and I felt ten stories tall every time someone would compliment my new vehicle.

I even rode it to school sometimes. Twenty-five miles. Both ways. One afternoon, I arrived home a little later than usual and was met outside on the street by L.A., his stepfather, Bobby, and my brother, Andre. They seemed to be creating a barrier between me and the house.

"What y'all d-d-d-d-doin'?" I stuttered, still out of breath from the ride.

"It's your Mama," Bobby said and took a step toward me. "The ambulance just took her away, Alton. They think she had a heart attack."

* * *

Mama had, in fact, had a massive heart attack and a minor stroke while sitting in the kitchen at our house. After a lifetime of working harder than anyone I knew—backbreaking work in the fields, at our house, and now in other people's houses; not to mention birthing twelve kids—her heart stopped working while she sat at the kitchen table, drinking a glass of lemonade.

The paramedics got to her in time to get her heart pumping again, but it was very weak and couldn't beat on its own. She stayed in the hospital for almost ninety days. The rest of us had to go on with life as if nothing had happened. The threat of social services coming in and splitting us up made us all swear to secrecy to the fact that our Mama was on life support in Louisville.

My sister, Toni, had been living with her boyfriend in Grand Rapids, Michigan, for the last several months, but agreed to come stay with me and my brothers until Mama could come home.

I prayed for Mama. I beseeched God to heal her. I was in church every minute the doors were open, and I fell on my knees every chance I got. The days became weeks and the weeks became months. Three months.

But this was not a particularly bad time. Not for me, anyway. I missed Mama when she wasn't there, but her absence was strangely empowering. Not only was I spending more time with my friends and getting closer to them and their families—they brought me in, fed me, made sure I was taken care of, and got me to wherever I needed to be when "White Lightning" wasn't enough—I was also getting closer to God. In some ways, Mama's heart attack helped my heart grow. Her absence allowed me to grow up. I was coming into my own and starting to gain confidence—in myself and in the places God was allowing me to be.

Then she came home.

She was hooked up to an oxygen tank at all times; tubes were sticking out of her nose, and she was extremely weak. She was so tired. Meanwhile, the bills were piling up. The power to our house had been disconnected more times than we could count. And we had no food.

"Alton, grab yo' brothers and come here to me," she called out from her bedroom. "Come on, now."

The next few minutes are a blur, even now. Her mouth was moving, but I couldn't make out the words. I couldn't understand what she was saying. Vernon, Charles, and Niles were crying. Andre got up and ran out of the room. After she was done talking, Mama just sat in her chair, breathed deep from the oxygen mask affixed to her face, and stared at me. "I can't do it no more, Alton. I'm done," she said. "You gots to go home." What Mama had been telling us over those lost minutes was that she couldn't care for us anymore.

Social services was going to get involved if we didn't pack up and go back to Alabama. Back to our father. Back to Sardis. Backwards.

I fell to my knees and cried. I prayed out loud and screamed until I made myself sick. Dry heaving and groaning, I fell facedown at my mother's feet and begged her not to send me back.

"What if I lived with L.A. and Anthony? What about Marvin, or Pooh? Could someone from church take us in?"

"Gots to be family," Mama mumbled as she looked away, expressionless. Emotionless.

Family?

The people in Newburg were my family. Bobby Carr was more of a father to me than the man in Selma could ever be. My friends were more like brothers than my own blood. The old ladies at church who gave me doughnuts and cookies were more involved and showed me more love than Mama Fat ever had. There was nothing for me in Alabama. And there was no way I would ever go back there.

"Gots to be family," Mama said again.

I lifted my eyes to meet hers. Tears now glistened on her cheeks and knowingly, lovingly, she tilted her head as if to say, "I know, baby. I know."

"Wuh-wuh-wuh-what about T-t-t-t-toooooooni?"

The words left my body before I even considered them.

What about Toni?
She's family!
She's an adult.
She even has kids of her own now!
She's a mom.
What about Toni?

Thirty-six hours later, I shakily ascended the formidable steps of a Greyhound Bus, dobbage tag slung over my shoulder, and unceremoniously left everything I had ever loved. Everything I ever longed for.

I didn't get to take my bike.

I didn't even say goodbye to L.A.

PART THREE

A CALL IN THE WILDERNESS

November 1983

* * *

I arrived in Grand Rapids just after 2 a.m. Standing water and piles of trash lined the streets where the homeless and drunkards slept and prostitutes seemed to sleepwalk to their next obligation. It was bitter cold—a type of freezing I'd never felt before. We used to get cold weather every once in a while back in Newburg, and temperatures would certainly fall below freezing, but that was January and February, never before Thanksgiving.

And the wind was different, too. It penetrated, deep, like it was angry and on a mission, and it brought a sting that could last for days and days.

I stepped down from the bus stairs wearing just a long-sleeved T-shirt and a pair of blue jeans that Andre had handed down, just as Ronald or Donald or Russell—or all three—had done for him. Looking around for Toni, I was met with an overwhelming sense of fear. I was sixteen years old. I was exhausted. I was alone. And I was one-hundred-percent sure that I was going to freeze to death on those filthy streets.

"Hey, boy!" A calm, baritone voice called to me from the shadows of the bus station. "You Alton?"

"Y-y-y-es, suh." I tried to stand tall as the voice took shape and a smiling face met mine. The man couldn't have been more than a couple of years older than me.

"First of all, welcome to Michigan," he said. "Second, you ain't got to call me 'sir.' Name's James. Toni's at home with the babies. You hungry?"

Toni's boyfriend, James, was good-looking and always smiling. He reminded me a lot of L.A., actually. They both had a way about them—a confidence that is evidently reserved for light-skinned Black folks with big, white teeth.

On the way to their apartment, James took me to White Castle and bought me six hamburgers. I hadn't eaten in two days, so I almost squealed out loud when he handed me that big, white sack of tiny, squared-off meat snacks.

Maybe Grand Rapids was gonna be alright after all.

* * *

My first few days in Michigan were uneventful. I didn't even leave the apartment. Toni had three small kids in the apartment. Two—a boy and a girl—from previous relationships, and another, the baby, with James. She made it pretty clear from day one that I would need to help watch the babies if I was going to stay there. I was happy to do this, because that meant I didn't have to build relationships with anyone else.

I preferred to be alone, and I was, more often than not. Plus, Toni and James lived in a rough part of town—the Southeast, off of Madison Avenue—and I was terrified to be out there on my own. When folks hear "Madison Avenue," they usually think about the famous street in New York City where advertising agencies once ruled the world, and luxury boutiques, restaurants, and hotels welcome the wealthy to indulge in extravagances most people in the world cannot even begin to dream about.

This was not that.

This Madison Avenue is where dreams go to die—in the dark, yet wide-awake reality of poverty, hopelessness, and despair. Madison Avenue was a scary place with very little to offer anyone, except for an address where creditors could send their notice. I was always amazed at the amount of mail Toni got every day.

"Maybe if they would stop sending letters all the time," she said one day, "they could afford to cut me a break!" It's a wonder that our power only got cut off a handful of times while I lived there. Somehow, Toni always found a way to pay for what we needed.

The apartment sat on the second floor of a three-story building. It had two bedrooms and one bathroom. The toilet, sink, and shower were covered in filth, despite our best efforts to scrub them clean. The floors throughout were all a cream-colored linoleum, stained with the history of others who undoubtedly used the space for hustling, dealing, and prostitution. The walls in the front room were a dark yellow—the effect of thousands of burned cigarettes. That's where I slept—on the couch in the front room. For the most part, the apartment was a soiled, but blank canvas.

We only had dry cereal at the apartment. Cheerios. It was cheap. It could keep. And even when Cheerios go stale, you can eat them and not tell much of a difference. Even the babies could eat them.

If you look up the word *poverty* in the dictionary, you'll get a pretty clear meaning: *the state of being extremely poor; the state of being inferior in quality or insufficient in amount*, and that makes perfect sense. But the idea of poverty can't be captured in a few words. It must be experienced to be believed. Then again, I was living the very definition of the word and I had no idea.

Does the fish ever know it's in water?

There was a small, Black-owned grocery store about 300 yards from the front steps of our apartment. I would run there and back when Toni or James needed milk or cereal or cigarettes. It was a poorly veiled secret that Mr. Walker was madly in love with Toni. All she had to do was smile and wave every now and then and he'd let me take whatever she needed. "Tell that sister of yours she owes me a kiss," he'd say, then wink and wave me away. I never could tell if he was a nice, old man or a dirty one, but he kept us from starving more times than I can count, so it didn't matter much to us.

Even closer, in the other direction, was a night club called O'Reilly's. I don't know where that name came from, because I never saw a single white person anywhere near that place, and I've never met a Black Irishman in my life. O'Reilly's was a violent hole-in-the-wall. It was known throughout the Southeast side of town as the place to go to get hookers, drugs, or dead, and I was terrified to walk past it. Down from there, though, was Madison Square Christian Reformed Church. I missed going to church. I was desperate for that feeling of belonging, of being known. I was desperate for those doughnuts. When I wasn't crying myself to sleep at night, I would lie on the floor at Toni's and sing to myself: *Soon and very soon ... we are going to see the King.*

But I couldn't ever bring myself to go in the church.

I was mad at God. I missed my friends. God gave me my best friends, and then He took them from me. God gave me a house and a neighborhood that I loved, and then He took them away. God showed me Himself in Louisville, and He was nowhere to be found in Grand Rapids. In His place were gunshots, the smell of rotten garbage, homelessness, and drug dealers.

I'd lost everything. Again.

* * *

After about a week, Toni took me to Union High School to transfer my records from Louisville. I didn't have a coat. I didn't have a sweater, or a hat, or gloves, or mittens. I didn't have a pair of boots, either. One of the first things I noticed when I walked down the halls was that everyone wore boots. And I mean everyone. Even the janitor was wearing galoshes and a scarf.

I was abhorrent. I probably smelled awful. I had terrible hygiene. I rarely brushed my teeth, and never wore deodorant. I didn't have anything of worth. I was just a skinny kid from Sardis by way of Louisville, and the only thing I brought with me to this frozen tundra—literally and figuratively—was the way I talked.

And I talked different.

Toni stayed right by my side as the assistant principal guided us down the hallway to first period. Memories of my first day at Newburg flooded me, and I felt myself about to explode with emotion. Toni could see the panic on my face and started walking a bit slower to create separation between us and our guide. She squeezed my hand and whispered, *"Let's go get you a coat after school, okay? Maybe a new shirt? Long sleeves, okay? This 'gon be alright, Alton. You 'gon like it here."*

As we stood at the back of my first-period class, which had already started, my eyes were wet with tears about to fall, until they met the gaze of the most beautiful girl I had ever seen. Yvonne. This wasn't a love-at-first-sight situation, although the feeling I had in that moment was something I had never felt before. There was a kindness in her eyes, a sparkle when she squinted and smiled that made every ounce of anxiety drain from my body. There was an empty desk next to hers, and with a sideways nod, she invited me to sit down. I'm not sure when Toni ended up leaving the classroom that morning because I never looked back.

Yvonne invited me to lunch later in the day and even helped me get to my next three classes. I didn't understand why she liked me, but I didn't ask any questions. I could have easily fallen in love with

Yvonne and asked her to marry me right there in the sophomore hall, but she didn't see me that way. She just *saw* me. She knew that I needed a friend, and she was willing to be that for me, even if it cost her disgusted whispers and gossip throughout the school. Yvonne was kind to me.

My life was pretty much the same routine in the months that followed: I'd wake up, put on a varied combination of the three shirts, two sweaters, and solitary pair of jeans that I owned, catch the bus, frantically look for Yvonne on the school lawn, and then walk with her to class.

After school, I would take the lonely bus back to the Southeast Side and hole up in the apartment, where I would spend all of my time looking after my niece and nephews. I had no friends. I had no hobbies. And I had nothing to look forward to, except Yvonne's smile each day at school. I was crawling deeper and deeper into the shell I thought I had broken out of and left in Louisville, but the walls were building, even higher than before.

* * *

Union High School was, of course, integrated by 1983, but that didn't mean anyone had to like it. Similar to our situation in Louisville, the poor, Southeast Side Black kids were bused to the mostly white and prominent suburbs on the West Side near Union.

Racial tensions were extremely high. I was spit on in the halls at school by white guys, pushed into lockers, called "nigger" more times than I can count, and told every day that I didn't belong. I agreed with them. I didn't belong there. I wanted to go back to Louisville where at least I knew I had people who loved me.

The bathrooms were not segregated, but it was common

knowledge that Black kids shouldn't venture into one of them alone. I heard way too many stories of both guys and girls who were tortured, humiliated, and even beaten for using the same toilets as the white students. I got very good at holding my bladder and bowels from 7:00 a.m. to 3:00 p.m.

I would almost wet my pants every day on the bus ride home from school. Sitting alone on the bus, I would wriggle and writhe until I was finally able to sprint home from the bus stop. Sometimes, I didn't quite make it, so I would have to wash my soiled jeans and underwear in the sink in order to have something to wear the next day.

Meanwhile, I was growing. From the time I stepped foot out of the Greyhound terminal eighteen months earlier, I had grown nearly eight inches.

*　*　*

I didn't have athletic shoes. I wore a size 13, and boats that big weren't easy to find. The only pair of shoes I owned were a pair of slip-on loafers and some too-small rain boots that Toni found at a consignment store.

Toni kicked James out of the apartment after he got laid off from his job one afternoon and proceeded to take out his disappointment on her. Within a month or two, she had another live-in boyfriend. He was no good at all. He treated Toni terribly and seemed to only endure me being around because I was bigger than him.

He barged into the apartment one night and threw a pair of old high-top Converse at me. They had obviously seen lots of time on the court.

"Maybe these can help you get the hell out of here, little man." He took a long drag from his cigarette and motioned for me to take the shoes. They were size 11, but I curled my toes and laced them up immediately.

He exhaled. "You ought to get out and play ball or something. Go to The Phillips and jump in a game."

The next morning, I entered the Paul I. Phillips facility for the first time. "The Phillips," as it was known throughout Grand Rapids, was a community gymnasium where the guys from my neighborhood and close-by projects would gather to play pick-up basketball and hit on girls. Everybody went to The Phillips. I had never played a legitimate game of basketball in my life, but I had always wanted to try. Before leaving Newburg, Marvin and L. A. had convinced me to try out for the basketball team, but I left before I ever got the chance. Until now. There I was, a country boy come to town, standing alone at the edge of the court bouncing a ball up and down, desperately trying not to stand out—but desperate to be noticed.

I found an empty goal on the far side of the facility and stood under it, gently pushing the ball upwards toward the opening of the net. Over and over, I would hop and push the ball up and in, up and in. Every once in a while, I would look up to see if anyone was watching. *Nope.* So, I kept shooting. I probably shot 150 two-handed layups before I tried adding dribbling to the routine: *Bounce, bounce, step, jump ...*

My legs took me higher than I expected, and suddenly the awkward two-handed layup turned into a two-handed dunk! I did it again. And again. I moved back a few steps after every successful try and did it again. I was having so much fun, I didn't even notice that the group behind me had stopped their game. When I finally looked up, they moved in closer and one of the players asked my name.

I was out of breath, but smiling—wholly impressed and happy with my new skill. "Alton," I managed to push out between breaths.

"Oh, you're that kid from Louisville, ain't ya?"

I nodded.

"You play ball?"

I shrugged.

"You don't know, or you ain't sayin'?"

The group behind him laughed.

"I've never really p-p-p-played b-b-before," I managed to reply.

"You're from Louisville, and you don't play ball?"

The 1982 Louisville Cardinal basketball team was led by legendary coach, Denny Crum, and the team was essentially unbeatable until they met Houston in the Final Four. Louisville was known for great basketball.

"You're from Louisville, and you don't play?" he asked again. For a split second, I thought about telling these guys about L.A. and Pooh and Marvin and the boys in Newburg, and how we made up an even *better* game than basketball back in the old neighborhood, but my better wits got a hold of me, and I held off on mentioning curb-ball.

"I don't believe you." He looked around at his friends and bounced a ball my way. "Let me see that dunk again."

Something changed inside me when I caught the ball. I didn't say a word. I turned around, leaned toward the basket, took one bounce, one step, and then jumped. I don't even remember putting the ball in the hoop, just the uproar around me. All of the players were jumping up and down, laughing, giving each other high-fives, and running toward me like I had just hit a half-court buzzer beater to win the state championship.

After a few more slams, the show was over and all of the players promised "same time tomorrow," then trickled out of the gym, one by one.

But I stayed. Dunk after dunk after lay-up after shot: Free throws, mid-range jump shots, long shots, and any other way I could find to try and put the ball in the basket. I had no idea what I was doing. I had no idea if I was shooting the ball properly or if some of the shots I was taking would even be allowed in "real basketball," but I didn't care. It was the most fun I had ever had.

The next day, I was already waiting as they opened the front doors of The Phillips at 7 a.m. Every other day that summer was the same thing. From open to close, I was playing ball and becoming known by others in the community as "that kid from Louisville." By the time school started back in August for my senior year, nobody called me Alton. My name was "Louie."

Even Yvonne met me on the first day of school and looked up at my wide eyes. "My, oh, my," she smiled. "Louie got big."

*　*　*

When I wasn't at school or playing pick-up games at The Phillips, I was babysitting for Toni. The new boyfriend was long gone by this time, because Toni was pregnant again. The day he found out, he went out to buy a pack of cigarettes and never came back. He even left his clothes, which turned out to be a good thing for me. Toni is the strongest person I have ever met. She was always positive, always looking for the silver lining in any situation, always thinking of others before herself. And she was a great mother to her kids.

But her life was difficult. I can't imagine the internal struggles a single mother in the projects has to deal with while trying to provide for and protect the people she loves from the external forces that constantly pit against her.

How am I supposed to feed these people?
How can I make sure they are safe?
Are they getting enough nutrition?
Do I have enough diapers?
Why does the baby cry all the time?
How can I make more money?
What about Alton?
Is he okay?
Who can help me?

She tried to kill herself on a Tuesday. I remember the day, because I was looking forward to playing ball at The Phillips after school. A few of us from Union had challenged a group from Ottawa Hills, a rival school nearby.

She took a handful of pills, laid down next to her crying baby, and fell asleep. When the neighbor found her, she had miraculously vomited most of the poison and still had a pulse, weak as it was. She spent the night in the hospital and was back at the apartment before I left for school. She didn't talk about it. We didn't even discuss the previous day. She just asked me if I had enough to eat for lunch, squeezed my arm, and started picking up the previous day's mess: toys, baby clothes, empty food containers, and my shoes. "Remind me to take you shopping," she said, quietly. "These things are probably two sizes too small." Three, but who's counting?

Less than a week later, Mama showed up with my brothers, Vernon, Charles, and Niles.

I didn't know how much I had missed Mama until I saw her face, heard her voice, felt her touch. She had come to help Toni, but truth be told, after a few days these visitors were more of a burden than a help. To me, anyway. Mama had never fully recovered from her heart attack, so she moved slowly and needed a lot of help getting from place to place, even in our tiny apartment. Toni let Mama take over her bedroom, so Toni was relegated to the kids' room. And my brothers slept on the floor next to me.

As frustrated as I was at their imposition, Toni seemed to love the chaos. Her smile even came back. Mama helped with the kids and even helped with buying groceries and cooking dinners.

The apartment was obviously too small for nine people—Toni, the three babies, me … and our four new *visitors* from Louisville—so we moved to a rundown house a few blocks from Madison Avenue a month later. It wasn't much bigger, but it had an extra room.

Having Mama at the house every day meant my babysitting duties were all but taken care of. I could come and go as I pleased, and that's exactly what I did. I was at The Phillips every time the doors were open, and I actually started doing pretty well in school. I wasn't a great student, but I was getting by with better than average marks. Never high enough for the Dean's List, but not so low as to be on any other lists, either.

I wasn't a part of a specific group of friends, but pretty much everybody knew who "Louie" was, and I started to feel more welcomed in social situations. More than likely, I was accepted by others because Yvonne still held me close and let me sit with her at lunch.

Everybody liked Yvonne, especially the male portion of everybody, but she never had a boyfriend. She was a devout Jehovah's

Witness, and that scared the bejeezus out of most would-be suitors. Jehovah's Witnesses believe that dating is only for people who want to get married, and that marriage is a permanent union. Yvonne was steadfast and let everybody know it, and that was usually enough to get guys looking past the fact that she was the most beautiful girl in school.

After lunch one day, I spent my free period in the school's gymnasium, shooting around and wasting time before math. There were only a couple of others there at the time, so when Coach Lloyd Kilgore called out, I knew he was talking to me.

"Where are you supposed to be?" he asked.

"Oh, I'm s-s-s-s-sorry, Coach. I-I-I-I'll llllleave."

"Hold on, now. I didn't say you had to leave. I asked, 'Where are you supposed to be?'" He smiled and moved in closer.

I was frozen with fear. "This is my free p-p-p-period. I-I-I'll go to ssssstudy hall. Study hall."

"Do you need to study? Do you have a test or something?"

"N-n-naw, suh."

"Okay." He stepped even closer. "Well, then, maybe you're supposed to be right here."

"Sir?" I was genuinely confused.

"You like basketball?" he asked.

"I don't rrrrreally p-p-play. I mean, I play at The-the-the Phiiiiiillips."

He cocked his head to the left a little: "You always talk like that?"

"I-I-I'm sorry. I don't t-t-t-t-alk good."

"It's all good. You're good. You're the kid they call Louie, ain't ya?"

He knew my name?

"Yes, suh." You could have knocked me over with a sneeze.

"What's your *real* name?"

"Alton Ha-hardy."

"Alton. Okay. So, do you like to play basketball?" He enunciated like I was hard of hearing or *special*.

"Yes, suh."

He turned and picked up the ball at his feet and bounced it between his legs as he started walking away. "Varsity tryouts are a week from today," he called back over his shoulder. "I expect you to be there," he paused, "Alton Hardy."

He knew my name.

* * *

Making the Union High School basketball team was a bigger deal than I even realized at the time. I had no frame of reference— no reason to think of my acceptance into this group as anything other than a step up, socially. But it wasn't a step up. It was an astronomical leap into a whole new world of being seen, known, appreciated, and even celebrated as an individual; and as a part of something ... *different.*

I was a Red Hawk.

It took about three weeks of grueling, humiliating practices for me to even begin learning the rules of the game; simple things like double-dribbling, traveling, three seconds in the paint, boxing out, and even free throws. I must have seemed like a rabid gorilla those first few days. All I knew to do was chase after the ball, grab it, and throw it to someone else. Anyone else. Pass. Run. Fight. Jump. Repeat. That's all I knew how to do, but I could do *all* of those things really well. Especially jumping. I was a rebounding machine.

I somehow found my way into the starting line-up as the season began. When I was off the court, I was still the lonely, alone, quiet, shy, and awkward kid that couldn't string more than three words together without sounding like a scratched record; but on the court, I was someone and something completely different. I was fast, strong, and dangerous. I took it personally when the other team had the ball—like a prizefighter demanding an apology. No one wanted to win more than I did. No one played harder. No one jumped higher. And no one had the slightest clue that I was scared to death most of the time.

We won our first sixteen ballgames by an average of thirty-four points, mostly due to Pop Simms.

Michael "Pop" Simms was the coolest guy I had ever met—even a step above L.A. He just had this way about him. Like something in the air around him allowed him to float above the rest of us. I was taller than Pops by more than four inches, but I always felt like I was looking up at him. He glided up and down the court with that basketball magically connected to his fingertips, until he decided to set it free. And his passes were a thing of beauty, too. So quick. So perfect. So true. His entire existence was effortless.

He wasn't trudging through life like me; he was flying. Pops never even touched the ground.

* * *

Newspaper headlines announced our team's victories:

Red Hawks stay Red Hot with "Pop";
Simms Leads Union to Victory (again);
Union Red Hawks fly high on the wings of "Pop" Simms;
And my all-time favorite: *"Pop" goes the Red Hawks.*

We were a sight to behold. Our colors were red and white, but at home, we came out red on red on red on red: red jerseys, red shorts, red socks, and bright-red Jaclar high tops. Those shoes would become the prologue to the legend that we would write together that season. Wherever we went, people throughout Madison and Grand Rapids recognized us as set apart. We were Red Hawks. Plus, nobody else would have had the confidence back in those days to wear shoes that outrageous.

All we had to do was walk down the street, and folks would stop, smile, clap, pat us on the back, or call out, "Go Hawks!"

Even when I was alone, people started noticing me. At the library. At the bus stop. Even at McDonald's: "You're Louie, right? Don't you play power forward with Pop and them? Here ... these cheeseburgers are on the house."

I ate for free at almost every fast-food restaurant near Madison that year. McDonalds's, White Castle, Burger King. All I had to do was feed Pop the ball on Tuesday and Friday nights, and the restaurants would feed me the other days.

I felt like a celebrity, and I suppose I was.

Pop and I became very close. The entire team was closely knit, but I'd follow Pop around like a hungry, little puppy dog. His confidence was catching, though, and I felt like I could do or say anything I wanted when I was with him. I could go anywhere and be treated like royalty. Even the white kids respected us.

Before joining the team, I would hear the word "nigger" almost every day. But Pop and basketball changed all of that. People didn't see a poor, Black kid from the ghetto. They saw Pop's wingman. And we flew everywhere together.

December 1983

* * *

I came home from practice on a cold, dark afternoon and was met by Mama at the front stoop. "We need to talk, baby boy." She grabbed me by the shoulder and ushered me inside.

Baby boy? This can't be good.

My immediate thought was that my father had died back in Selma, or something had happened to one of my brothers.

"You are not going to understand this," she said with tears forming in her big, black eyes, "but we need to get out of here."

Mama was miserable in Grand Rapids. It was so sad to see her try and navigate those cold streets. Her heart attack had aged her twenty years, and she simply couldn't exist like that anymore. "I've been talking with Toni, and she don't want to be here, either. Too many bad memories ... You know, with the accident."

Mama never could come to grips with the fact that Toni had wanted to kill herself. She always referred to her suicide attempt as *the accident.*

"I know you got your friends here, baby boy, but we got to get out of Michigan."

Those words hit me with the force of a steam engine. *We got to get out of Michigan.* Everything she said after that was a muffled blur.

She and Toni were taking the babies and moving to Buffalo, where my oldest sister, Doris, and her family had been living for the past two years. Vernon and Charles had decided to go back to

Selma to live with my father. As toxic as that place had been for me less than a decade ago, Selma held fond memories for my brothers. They were headed South.

Her announcement—that we were leaving Michigan—broke me to the point of weeping.

> *I can't do this again.*
> *I can't leave my friends.*
> *I can't start over.*
> *I can't do it.*
> *I won't.*

I ran from the house as fast as I could—weeping, crying out to God, and replaying Mama's words over and over in my head. I didn't have a planned destination; I just ran. My feet carried me to the only place I felt safe, the only place I knew I would find comfort. The Phillips was about to close for the night, but I made my way through the front doors and sneaked onto the court. For the next half hour, I crouched in the corner of the half-lit gymnasium, holding a basketball and weeping silently.

Alone.

When I arrived back at the house, I told Mama and Toni that I wasn't going with them. "Every time I get something g-g-good, I ha-ha-ha-have to l-l-l-leave it," I cried. "I'm not letting that ha-ha-happen again. I don't care what I ha-a-a-a-ve to d-do. I'll sleep at the school if I have to, but I'm n-n-n-not l-l-l-leaving here."

Mama cried and put up a fight, but Toni understood. She had seen me grow up over the past year and a half. She knew how important my friends, the team, and that place had been for me.

Mama, Vernon, and Toni packed their things and readied to leave Grand Rapids. Mama somehow got in touch with my brother

Ronald, who was—as he put it—between jobs and ready to start something new. He committed to taking over the rent on Paris Street and promised to help me get through my senior year of high school. He was living in Des Moines, Iowa, at the time, and figured he could easily trade one winter weather nightmare for another.

A week later, ten days before Christmas, Mama and Toni and the kids were gone. Three days after that, Ronald sent a message that he had found another job in Des Moines and wouldn't be moving to Grand Rapids after all. "Don't tell Mama just yet," he said. "We don't need to worry her with this right before Christmas."

I spent the next ten weeks alone in that house. The power company cut off service around the middle of January. The gas and water went next. I woke up every morning and rushed to the school locker room to shower and get ready for school. After practice or games, I would alternate among McDonald's, Burger King, and wherever else a free meal could be found. Then, I would rush to The Phillips to try and get warm before heading back into the cold, dark, empty house where I would rock myself to sleep wearing every piece of clothing I could find. When the cold became unbearable, I would bundle up best I could and run up and down the street behind the house to at least keep blood moving to my head, hands, and feet.

It was so cold.

I remember thinking that everything I had heard about hell had to be wrong. *Eternal damnation in fire could never be as bad as this.*

Somehow, my living conditions didn't affect my game. The Red Hawks were continuing to dominate every opponent we faced, and I was racking up rebounds and points at the same trajectory as the standouts on our team—even Pop. I looked forward to away games the most, because I got to spend more time with my teammates and coaches. We would travel together, eat together, win together, and celebrate together in the warmth of a charter bus. When we weren't on the road, most of my teammates were picking up girls.

Pop had a girlfriend for every day of the week, and would tease me:
Louie, you don't like girls?
What's the matter, Louie? You afraid of women?

Of course I liked girls, and of course I was one-hundred percent afraid of them, but that's not why I didn't go out. I didn't have any money. I didn't have a winter coat. I didn't even have another pair of shoes. It was better for me to just go to The Phillips and go home.

But home was becoming more and more unbearable. Temperatures were consistently below zero degrees, and I could find no relief after sundown. No amount of blankets, pairs of socks, layers of T-shirts, or even sweatshirts and sweatpants could protect me from the sting of winter.

One night, I couldn't stand it anymore. Every part of my body was in intense pain. I had to move. I had to get out of there. Snow was pouring with a vengeance. Brown, bespattered piles lined the streets, gathering inch after inch, creating mountains of ice all around me. I broke out of the front door and started to run. I was slipping and falling and crying out for God to save me. "Jesus, I need you," I wept. "Please help me. Please, Jesus. Please, Jesus. Please."

I don't know how far I ran or how long I was outside, but the sun was breaking over the horizon as I made it back home, tears literally frozen to my face.

I went inside, grabbed my books, took off a few layers of wet clothes, and went straight to school.

That afternoon after practice, the assistant coach, Elmo Carlisle, approached me: "Louie, I'm taking you home tonight. You don't need to be walking home in that storm." The snow and ice had been gathering all day, making it impossible to travel on foot. Coach 'Mo lived three houses down from me on Paris Street and would offer to give me a lift from time to time, but that night he didn't give me a choice. The ride home was more uncomfortable than the walk would have been.

He drove slow, and his eyes never left mine when he asked:

> *"What's going on with you, Louie?*
> *Where is your family?*
> *Why is your house always so dark?*
> *Why don't I ever see your Mama no more?*
> *Are you okay?*
> *Are you alone?"*

Great big tears pooled and then fell heavy on my cheeks.

> *"Have you been living in that house by yourself?"*

Like a dam that had reached its weight, my emotions let loose and I began weeping in 'Mo's car. I told him everything. The past year and a half came rushing out, and I folded over in the passenger's seat like an empty suit. I explained how I refused to go with my family to Buffalo, how I couldn't leave my team, my friends, my life.

Elmo could be a scary guy. He was kind, but rough around the edges. No-nonsense. And he could put the fear of God in you with a glare from the sidelines, or through the barrage of curse words that seemed to come more naturally to him than breathing. That night, though—during that short car ride—he softened. He rested his huge hand on my back the entire way home and let me know that he was going to keep me safe.

We turned onto Paris Street, and he didn't even slow down when we passed my house. "You don't have to be alone no more," he whispered, and then pulled into his driveway.

* * *

Elmo wasn't married. He lived with his mother, Big Ma, and an array of other family members who seemed to come and go with the sun. Big Ma was the kindest, most generous woman I had ever met. She never even questioned who I was when we entered the front door. She simply took my backpack from my slumped shoulders and told me to sit. "I've got sugar cookies and milk. You sit yo skinny self down and let Big Ma fatten you up some."

I was overwhelmed at first—mostly because of the heat in the room. It was warm, almost too warm, but within two minutes, I was completely thawed and as relaxed as I had been in years. I must've eaten fifteen cookies before finally drifting to sleep. That was the first time I remember sleeping in an actual bed, not just a mattress on the floor, on couch cushions, or on a pile of dirty clothes.

The next morning, Elmo woke me with a shove and grunted, "Breakfast" before walking out of the room. I heard his huge footsteps descend the stairs and the front door close heavy behind them.

Big Ma was in the kitchen—she was always in the kitchen—making biscuits and gravy for breakfast. Ma was originally from Brandon, Mississippi, and her Southern roots and recipes ran deep. She had the most genuine, warm, and bright white smile. She flashed it wide as she delivered my food. "Eat up, baby. Lucille will be here in a few minutes to run you to school."

Lucille Carlisle, Elmo's older sister, lived a few blocks over from Paris Street with her son, Boochie, who was a few years younger than me. She didn't want Boochie riding the school bus all the way to town, so she would take him to school and pick him up every day.

Lucille, a tiny woman with bright, bleached-blonde hair, busted in the back door near the kitchen with a familiar smile and huge, happy eyes: "Oooh, Big Ma, you cooking biscuits!" She let out a laugh and hugged Ma around the waist. She turned her attention to me and, with hands on hips, cocked her head and smiled, "And you must be Louie!" She walked toward me with her arms outstretched like she was going to give me a hug, but I backed away—a bit stunned by her electricity. I smiled back, "Oh, y-y-y-yes, ma'am."

Her laugh was bigger than she was. "Did you hear that, Ma? This boy called me 'ma'am.' Sweetheart, I ain't old enough for 'Ma'am.' You best call me Lucille before you hurt my feelings!"

She laughed again and told me to grab my books. "After school," she said, "we'll grab your stuff from down the street and you can keep it at my house. We 'gon be good friends, Louie!" She laughed again and hugged Big Ma goodbye. "Louie and Lucille! We were meant for each other ..." She grabbed a biscuit off the counter for Boochie and then bounced out the door and down the steps, almost skipping the whole way to her car. Big Ma could see that I was overwhelmed. "Here," she picked up my plate, "you can take this with you. Just tell that crazy daughter of mine to bring it back to me when y'all come for dinner. I hope you like pork chops."

I didn't know whether to laugh, cry, jump for joy, or fall to my knees. *Was this even real?*

Elmo and Big Ma had told Lucille about me the night before, and she never hesitated to insist that I stay with her and her son. Lucille's house was almost the same size as Big Ma's, but with about four or five fewer people wandering in and out every day.

Over the next few weeks, when I wasn't on the basketball court, I was with Boochie. He loved spending time with me and the other players on Union's team, and they made him feel like a part of us—especially after learning that he was Elmo's nephew. Boochie and I became like brothers, and Lucille was quickly the Mom I never had: happy, loving, compassionate, thoughtful, interested, and engaged.

She made sure I did my homework every night. She made sure I was fed every day. She cheered at every basketball game. And she prayed with and for me.

I felt as though I had been praying for *her* my entire life. Ever since those lonely walks in the woods back in Sardis. Watching the trees and leaves dance in the wind, talking to the birds, reaching for arms to hold me, starving—not just for something to eat, but for the warmth I finally saw and felt in Lucille's eyes.

I never understood where the warmth, the kindness, or her endless depths of love came from—this tiny, Black lady who grew up in a place not much different from Sardis. This tiny, Black lady who once watched as a group of young white men beat an old Black man to death on the streets of Brandon, Mississippi. This tiny, Black lady who had been a victim of bigotry, violence, loneliness, and Blackness her whole life.

Where does that joy come from?
How did she find it?
How does she keep it?
And how can I show her how much I need it?

She cried the first time I called her Mom and said I didn't have to call her that. But I wanted to. I was desperate to. Meanwhile, the Red Hawks were unstoppable. We breezed through the regular season and playoffs without much competition at all. Pop was averaging more than thirty points per game. I had double digit rebounds every night, and I even had the chance to score some points every now and then.

We were the number-two ranked team in the state of Michigan behind Flint Northwestern, who happened to be the number-one ranked team in the nation. Their team was made up of Jeff Grayer, a 6'5" shooting guard who went on to play at Iowa State and the NBA; Glen Rice, a 6'8" small forward who later played at the University of Michigan before becoming a three-time NBA All-Star; and Andre Rison, who hung up his high-tops for football cleats at Michigan State, and then went on to play fifteen years in the NFL, where he was a five-time Pro Bowler and Super Bowl Champion.

When the Red Hawks and the Wildcats met in the quarterfinals, nobody really gave us a chance to win, but we took them to the wire, losing by just four points. I was devastated. I'm not sure what I thought winning the championship might get me, but I put everything into that game, so my heart and soul were crushed when the buzzer sounded and the Wildcats fans rushed the court. I fell to my knees and cried and pounded the court with my fists. Pop came to me and guided me to my feet. He seemed confused by my reaction and simply hugged me in the middle of the gym while the celebration continued around us. I was broken. I was terrified. I was about to be alone. Again.

Most of my Union teammates had plans for after high school. Not me. Pop was headed to play scholarship ball at Marquette University. He wanted me to go with him to Milwaukee, but I didn't have money for school or a place to live. Donnie was a football star, so he decided to stay close and play running back at Central Michigan. Even Brad and Rodney, who were two years younger than us, were committed to play ball in college. Rodney had family in California and walked on the basketball team at Santa Clara College. Brad went on to play basketball at Missouri.

A lot of kids would end up in places like Flint, Ann Arbor, Detroit, or Chicago, but most would stay close to home and live with their parents.

I didn't have parents. I had Lucille and Boochie, but my time at their home was coming to a quick end. My new Mom had prodigal sons of her own who were making their way back to shelter and food that spring. There was not going to be room for me after graduation. Mom never told me I had to leave, but I knew I was about to overstay my welcome. As much as I loved her and she loved me, I didn't feel like her house was my home.

> *Maybe I'll join the military …*
> *They have to feed you in the military, right?*
> *Maybe I'll go back to Louisville …*
> *I can stay with L.A. or Pooh …*
> *I can find my old friends …*
> *I wonder if they found my bicycle …*

I had nowhere to go. No plan for the future. And no idea how to get from one day to the next.

I started isolating myself and spending time away from the house—playing pick-up games at The Phillips, or walking alone. I thought I was protecting myself from pain that seemed imminent, but I was really just hurting the one person in the world who showed me unconditional and enduring love. Unbeknownst to me, Lucille and Elmo had been working on a plan of their own.

Elmo used to play ball with the newly appointed head basketball coach at Alpena Community College. He convinced his old friend—solely on his word—to let me come play for him. I broke down and wept in Lucille's arms the Sunday afternoon they told me that I would be going to college. Lucille also presented me with a brand-new, gray suit and black patent leather, lace-up dress shoes so that I would have something nice to wear to my high school graduation.

When my name was called and I received my diploma, Lucille was there, standing, clapping, cheering, and crying as the poor, lonely boy she claimed as her own walked across the rickety stage and fell into her waiting arms.

*　*　*

Alpena Community College is about a four-hour drive north from Grand Rapids, and rests neatly on the brown, sandy banks of Lake Huron. Nothing at all like the inner-city streets of Grand Rapids, the cracker box neighborhoods of Louisville, or the dirt roads and cotton fields of Sardis, Alabama, from which I was only seven years removed.

Basketball players had to report to campus for early workouts a few weeks before classes started, and that turned out to be a great blessing. I hadn't registered for classes, picked a meal plan, signed up for a work study program, or completed any of the necessary paperwork for incoming freshmen. The only preparation I had done for my new life was to secure a new pair of Jaclar high tops by selling just about every piece of clothing I owned to a consignment shop the day before.

Elmo pulled up to the dormitory and helped me get my two boxes of belongings up the stairs to my third-floor room. He shook my hand and then turned to make the long journey home. Before leaving the room, he called back: "This is a gift, Louie. Don't waste this."

This is a gift. This is a gift. This is a gift. Those four words kept running through my head over and over, like the refrain of one of those moans Mama used to hum when she was sad.

There was supposed to be hope in those words, but I just felt dread.

The next few days were filled with so much information, rules, and overwhelming details, I found myself on the verge of panic attacks every moment I wasn't on the court with my new team. There, I felt safe. I knew what to do: *Go as hard as you can, as fast as you can; jump as high as you can; get the ball again and again and again; pass the ball; shoot the ball; repeat.* Off of the court, I might as well have been in a different country. I didn't know where anything was located. I didn't know the right questions to ask. And I certainly didn't know how to answer the registrar's questions:

> **Name:** Alton Hardy
>
> **Date of Birth:** August 8, 1966
>
> **Place of Birth:** Sardis, Alabama
>
> **Name of Hospital:** Hospital?
>
> **Social Security Number:** I don't think I have one of those.
>
> **Driver's License Number:** I don't know how to drive.
>
> **Parent Names:** Lucille Carlisle … No, wait. My *real* parents?
>
> **Intended Major:** I don't know.
>
> **Intended Minor:** I don't know.
>
> **Emergency Contact:** I'm not sure.
>
> **Home Phone:** We ne-ne-ver ha-ad a ph-phone.
>
> **Permanent Address:** C-c-can I c-c-c-all … Can I call my M-m-mom?

Classes hadn't even started, but I was already failing. My entire life had been about reacting to circumstance. Before that moment, I don't recall ever making an informed decision or a proactive choice about anything, ever. Life was something to be survived, not planned. At Alpena, I was being asked to think about my future, and I had no idea how to do that. I had never known a Black person to even go to college, much less dream about what's next. Those kinds of ponderings were meant for white people who become doctors or go to law school; men and women in suits and shiny shoes who work in the skyscrapers downtown.

School had always been a necessary chore, not a means to a better end. In fact, the smartest people I had ever known had second or third grade educations at best. I was determined to make Lucille and Elmo and everybody else proud of me, but being asked what I wanted to study was like asking a starving man what he wanted to eat. It didn't matter. Just tell me where the food is.

Basketball workouts were easy compared to Union. There were no stand-out stars on the team. No Pop Simms, to be sure. I quickly became a leader on the team, not because of my talent, but because I worked harder than anyone else. The fear of failure overruled any desire I had for the spotlight, but with one came the other.

I even got invited to parties—even white kids' parties off campus. But popularity wasn't natural for me. I didn't have very many friends growing up, but the relationships I had were deep. Here, I was role playing at best. My entire Alpena existence was motivated by fear; nothing real.

As the first semester was nearing its end, I was assigned a paper to write for my English class—*a thousand-word essay on a great writer from the twentieth century.*

For the next three weeks, I spent every available hour in the library—researching, reading, writing, re-writing, and even conjuring the courage to ask the librarian to read my rough drafts. Mrs. Schwartz was a profoundly kind person but played the part of librarian as though she were cast by Hollywood directors. She was a short, squatty lady with immovable, curly brown hair that resembled a dented motorcycle helmet. She secured her thin, rectangular spectacles with a gold link chain, and wore them at the very tip of her nose as she peered, head bowed, over a sea of students who dared not make a noise outside of turning pages.

There was a genuineness and depth to her smile that drew me to her from our very first interaction. I cannot adequately count the number of times I sought that smile, and her assistance, during that first semester.

After completing the third and final draft of my paper on Langston Hughes, the African American author and poet who was a central figure in the rise of Black artists during the 1920s, Mrs. Schwartz approached me with tears in her eyes.

She read aloud: *Hughes wrote about the joys and sorrows of ordinary Blacks. His poems and plays promoted equality and reconciliation, condemned racism and injustice, and celebrated African American culture, humor, and spirituality.*

"Alton, this is beautiful," she said. "I had no idea that Mr. Hughes was such an important writer. I marked a few grammatical and spelling errors, but you've done a wonderful job."

I almost floated out of that library.

After making my final changes, I turned in the paper and then rested for the first time in almost a month. It took over a week for my professor to grade the twenty-nine papers from my class, so my anticipation had built to the point of bursting. Upon handing me my paper, the professor said, "You should thank God for basketball, Mr. Hardy. I imagine that's the only reason you are still here. This is one of the worst papers I've ever read." He exhaled deeply, then continued, "And the assignment was to write a paper on a *great* writer, not a Black one."

At the top of the cover page, in bright red marker, was a circled D-. That was the only mark on the five-and-a-half stapled pages I had written. No comments. No suggestions. No explanations of grammatical or punctuation errors.

I was broken. Not only was I immediately reminded of the shortcomings I had worked so hard to overcome; my professor had just confirmed them. Upon exiting the classroom, I slammed through the double doors leading to the courtyard outside and vomited in the bushes that lined the building. The rush of adrenaline, disappointment, and heartache spewed out and left me heaving. Alone.

I made up my mind then and there that I would never try to do anything that required me to be "smart" ever again. I didn't have to be smart to play basketball. By this time, the game was second nature, and the playbook at Alpena consisted of only about four pages. The first three were leadership quotes and inspirational thoughts from John Wooden, John F. Kennedy, and other old, white men, and the plays drawn up by our coach were only slightly more defined than: *Go out there and score more points than the other guys.*

The court was the only place I felt at home, the only place I felt safe from the judgmental glances and disgusted glares of my classmates and professors.

Of course, that wasn't the truth I was experiencing, but it was the only truth I could hold onto, the only thing that could justify the darkness and loneliness I felt so deeply.

Christmas break brought a brand-new despair. The dorms were set to be closed between December 18 and January 4 when practice and classes would resume. I had nowhere to go. I hadn't spoken to or communicated with Mama, Toni, Doris, or any of my immediate family since arriving at Alpena. My new family, Lucille, Elmo, Big Ma, and Boochie, had extended family taking up every inch of bed, couch, or floor space in their homes. And I was too embarrassed to tell anyone on my team that I was homeless.

Mrs. Schwartz from the library smiled, handed me a candy cane wrapped with red and green ribbon, and asked, "Hey! How did your professor like your paper?"

I couldn't bear to tell her the truth, so I faked a grin, shrugged, and said, "He loved it. We did good, Mrs. S."

"Oh, that's so great, Alton. Congratulations! So, do you have any big plans for the holidays?"

I'm not sure if it was the lie I had just told her, or the lies I had started to believe about myself, but something caused the lump in my throat to swell, and great, big tears formed under my eyes.

She grabbed my arm and demanded that I sit and talk to her. I told her everything. She was amazed as I shared the details of moving from Louisville to Grand Rapids; the months I spent alone in the abandoned house on Paris Street; my new family who gave me the opportunity to go to college; and the truth about my English professor.

She wiped the tears from her cheeks and squeezed my hands. "You poor thing," she breathed. "Come with me."

I'll never know exactly how she managed to secure the hotel room, but that night—and for the next sixteen nights—I stayed for free at the Holiday Inn near campus, where I was able to eat for free in the lobby restaurant. I was alone that Christmas, but somehow felt safe.

Lonely, but loved. Alone, but seen.

* * *

The start of a new semester brought with it a new basketball season, and I was a man on a mission. What I lacked in the classroom, I more than made up for on the court. That season, I led the team in rebounds, blocks, assists, and scoring, coming up just short for the postseason, despite our nominal talent.

I made passing grades each semester, but never finished with more than a C-average. On breaks, I would either stay with teammates, or make the half-day bus ride to Grand Rapids to see Mom and Boochie before heading back to work out or endure another academic disappointment.

The next season was as glory-filled and disappointing as the first. I had great personal stats, but we failed to make the playoffs and our season ended before I had even considered what would happen next. As well as I had been playing, there weren't opportunities for me to go and play at a four-year school, and I certainly wasn't going to be drafted to play in the NBA.

I had to leave.

May 1987

*　*　*

Ronald finally made good on his promise from three years earlier and moved to Grand Rapids. He had a girlfriend, and they were living in a small two-bedroom near Madison. The house had an unfinished basement, which is where he allowed me to stay.

I went to see Lucille and Boochie almost every day, but the home that once saved my life now served as place of shelter and protection for others—namely Lucille's grown children and their spouses and children. I spent most of my time trying to relive my high school glory days at The Phillips, but that routine quickly lost its shine. I didn't have a car or a job or a plan. College had simply delayed the inevitable, and I was right back in the same desperate and despairing place I had been before—staring out at the same, dreadful reality before me, walking the same cold streets.

I prayed sometimes, but mostly as a vagrant might call out, begging for the jangle of a coin to ring the bottom of his cup. I didn't know what I needed; I just knew I didn't have it.

I didn't have much of anything. Most of my high school friends were either still in school, or they had dropped out and were working full-time. A few less motivated guys were still hanging out and playing ball at The Phillips every day, but I didn't see the point. Grown men still playing like kids without a care in the world. I'd pass them on the street, or see them hanging out at bus stops, drinking, smoking, and sometimes even asking passersby for a cigarette, some spare change, or worse.

Drugs had entered Grand Rapids pretty heavily by 1989, and for a lot of folks on the streets, crack cocaine was the easiest way to escape from the misery and monotony of hopelessness. I was scared to death of the stuff, scared of death, and I watched the news channels enough to know that crack was killing a lot of brothers and sisters from places like where I lived. Crime was also reaching toward an all-time high, but I didn't have a lot to worry about. Aside from the shirt on my back and the Goodwill pants covering my legs, I didn't have anything to take.

*　*　*

Ronald had been after me for a couple of months to get a job, but I had no car—I didn't even know how to drive. I had no dream, degree, or expertise in anything. I wasn't even qualified to clean the streets. "You got to either get a job, or go find Eddie in Saudi Arabia, or wherever the hell they got him these days." My oldest brother had joined the military a few years earlier and was evidently getting to see the whole world, by the sound of it.

"Alton, you can't stay here no more, man. You got to get your own place. You a grown man. Time to act like one."

A grown man? Me?

What does that even mean? How does a grown man act?

I thought back to the men in my life:

My father, the alcoholic sharecropper who dug graves and beat my mama; my brothers; Reverend Short; and Gene Sallie or Uncle Kidd, the witch doctors. I thought about the white men back in Sardis—Mr. Smith, Cade Collins, and the police who strung up Andre out front of our house. Were those men? Were they who was I was supposed to become? What about Bobby Carr? I could hardly remember what L.A.'s stepfather in Newburg looked like. He was kind. I remembered that. He loved his family. I remembered that, too.

But I didn't have a family

Toni's old boyfriends were men. But they all left. One by one. They all chose to go. What about Elmo and Coach Kilgore? Those men were men, right? But I wasn't like them. *Was I?*

I didn't know who I was supposed to be, how I was supposed to act, or what I was possibly qualified to do. All I knew for sure was that I had to get a job. Aside from the summer park gig I had a few months before leaving Newburg, I had never worked anywhere. People would give me five dollars for helping them move a couch or refrigerator. I'd sometimes get paid to clean up the parking lot in front of The Phillips, or sweep and mop behind the concessions stand, but those dollars were just enough to buy a candy bar or a 40-ounce of Olde English 800.

I was drinking at least two 40-ounce bottles of malt liquor every night, mostly because I was bored, but it also helped me sleep. When I was awake, I felt like I was in a dream, but every time I closed my eyes, my mind would race and I would be filled with overwhelming dread. The liquor helped keep my despondence at an even keel. I never sank too low, but my life was rudderless, and even if I had a paddle, I didn't know which way to row. One morning, I woke up earlier than normal and went for a walk. It was freezing. As the sun broke through the haze that hung heavy over Madison Square, it revealed to me things I had never paid much attention to. The streets were broken. Not just with potholes, cracked sidewalks, and other signs of neglect, but with people. Black people.

I saw drug deals—buying, selling, using; huddled mounds of humanity trying to keep warm over smoking steel drums; people sleeping in the doorways of abandoned buildings; and deranged men and women walking, shuffling, and even crawling to nowhere in particular. Sometimes they would be talking to themselves or laughing, or fist-fighting the air as if warding off the ghosts of a thousand years. I saw friends of mine waiting at bus stops, or riding bicycles—like twenty-year-old schoolboys pedaling off to avoid real life.

As I completed the circle around my block and approached the crosswalk that led me to Ronald's house, it hit me that these lives I was mourning, these people who were existing on the verge of death on those streets, were me.

I must have cried for two hours straight before managing the courage to ask Ronald to help me. I knew that if I was going to get out of his house and away from the future that waited for me out there, my two-year general studies degree wasn't going to do it, and basketball was never going to be my vehicle to bigger and better things.

I was going to have to learn how to drive.

Ronald found an old phone book and helped to identify six or eight numbers for driving schools. He said he would help me pay the $12.50 per lesson, "but you better not need more than one lesson, ya heard me?"

I heard him.

I went to the payphone just a few blocks away from Toni's old apartment—just up the street from O'Reilly's Pub and across from Madison Square Church—with a pocketful of change and started calling.

The first two numbers had been disconnected. The third answered:

Y-y-y-es, sir. I need drrrrr… I need driving l-lessons.

Okay, well, you've called the right place. What's your name, son?

Name's Al. Al-ton.

Okie-dokie, Al, nice to meet you. My name is Richard. You say you want driving lessons? How old of a young man are you?

Twenty years old.

Twenty?

Yes, sir.

… and you don't have your license, yet, Al? May I ask why not?

I never … I never tried before.

Well, that's alright, Al. It's never too late to try. Wherebouts do you live?

I'm at a p-p-p-pay phone. In Madisssssson. Can you p-p-p-pick m-m-m-me up?

There were a few seconds of silence before Richard cleared his throat and agreed to drive over from Burton Heights. "I go to church over there," he said. "I know exactly where you are. Sit tight, I'll be right over."

About thirty minutes later, an older white man slowly approached me in his silver 1981 Buick Century. I was still standing at the payphone, so he rolled down the passenger side window: "Are you Al?" he asked with a big smile.

"Yessir. I'm Alton Hardy."

"You must be freezing, Al. Hop in here! I've got the heat on."

I opened the passenger door, bent down, and ducked my head to lean in. "You're huge, Al!" He kind of laughed. "I mean, you're a full-grown man, aren't you?"

"Yessir," I feigned a smile in return.

Richard Vandenburg was a gentle, kind, and gracious man. He was so soft-spoken, I had a hard time understanding many of his instructions as we made our way through the maze of cars and traffic cones in the Madison Church parking lot.

"Turn here. That's good. Easy does it. Don't forget your turn signal. Very Nice. Ease up on the brake. There you go. Slowly. Perfect.

You're doing great, Al. Are you sure you've never done this before? Let's try that again. Bravo, kiddo. Good for you!"

We met for three days before Mr. Vandenburg suggested we take a real drive. "Let's take this show on the road … What do you say, Al? You ready? Ah! Of course you are," he continued.

Left on Madison Avenue. Right on Adams Street. Left on Eastern Avenue. Left on Hall Street. Left on Paris.

Paris Avenue. We made our way down my old street, passed my old house, and then slowed to a roll as we passed Big Ma and Elmo's. I was overcome with emotion, and silent tears fell from my cheeks to my shirt. "Hey, big guy. You okay?" My instructor's voice softened even more than usual. "Maybe it's time we head back," he whispered.

Upon entering the church parking lot, Richard told me to pull into a space that split two other vehicles. "This is your last test, young man. Let's see if you can bring this ship to port."

I slowly eased the Buick between the other cars, pressed on the brake, and then wrestled the gear shift into its top position. We both exhaled, and Richard smiled. He told me that I passed and then refused to take my money as we shook hands. "It was a real pleasure to meet you, Alton Hardy. You are a fine young man, and I hope to see you again soon, son."

His eyes were gleaming as he reached up and put his hand on my shoulder. "Don't drive too far away, okay? I'd love to see you in church some time." And with that, he handed me a few papers with his signature on them and told me where to go to get my driver's license.

* * *

Three months later, I found myself in the office of a man named Jim Hoover. Jim was a short, overweight, balding white man who wore short-sleeved dress shirts and big, thick neckties that almost never matched his too-short pants rising above white socks and black, no-slip dress shoes. He was an unsavory sight with a personality to match, and he reluctantly offered me a job in his warehouse at the Northwestern Beer Company.

"You'll get paid like everybody else," he said. "So there's no reason for you to ask for a raise or an advance or anything like that. I know you people always need more money ..."

I don't think I realized at the time that by "you people," he wasn't simply referring to those of us hired to crush bottles and cans. He meant people who looked like me, but I didn't care. I was going to get paid eight dollars an hour! More money than I had ever dreamt of having at one time. I could make almost a hundred dollars a day!

It just so happens that 1988 was an important year for the beer industry in Michigan. The International Brotherhood of Teamsters, Local 744, and the Chicago Beer Wholesalers Association were at odds about pay and overtime and various red-taped details I never could bring myself to care much about. While negotiations were happening, about 650 union members went on strike against the distributors, so I got hired. I didn't understand the strike. I didn't even know what the teamsters were. All I knew was I needed a job and they said, "Break these bottles, crush those cans, stack those boxes, and don't forget to clock out in the morning."

After a couple of months, Ronald had enough of me taking up residence on his sofa, so he gladly helped me find a one-bedroom apartment to rent. It was only 150 dollars per month, plus electric and gas, and it came with a small refrigerator and stove. Lucille gave me some dishes, a few forks and spoons from her kitchen, and even bought me a sleeper sofa from the Goodwill. It cost almost as much as my first month's rent, but she justified the expense because it was going to double as my bed until I could find a mattress that wasn't damaged or too badly soiled.

Lucille also took me to the bank and helped me open a checking account so I could get my utilities registered and in my name. I was so proud the first time I ever went to pay my power bill with a check that had my name printed on it. The receptionist thought I was high on drugs. "Ain't nobody come in here laughing," she said, eyes wide. "You better go on now 'fo I call the police!" She laughed, too, as I all but hop-skipped out of the lobby.

It wasn't long before Mr. Hoover promoted me to the loading floor where I'd stack pallets upon pallets of every beer brand imaginable—one after the other—onto the delivery trucks. This promotion also came with a dollar-fifty per hour pay raise, which put about 125 extra dollars in my bank account every week. It was hard work, but simple.

At this time, I was about as big and strong as I had ever been, so the labor, while intense at times, was nothing I couldn't handle with tolerable ease. I was working eighty- to- ninety-hour weeks, and was happy to do it. In fact, I actually enjoyed my time at the distribution center, except for when I was forced to work with "Newhart."

Newhart was a big, white guy—even bigger than me— and he hated Black people. Since I was the only Black person at Northwestern, I received the full brunt of his detestation, so I stayed away from him as much as possible. Some days, though, we would find ourselves working the same trucks or pallets, and that's when he would start in.

"I can't believe they've got me training monkeys," he'd say. "What do I look like, a damn zookeeper? Hey, monkey, the zoo is on the other side of town. Why don't you go on home ... Monkey." He always ended one of his rants with an exclamatory "Monkey" or "Boy" or "Nigger."

"You're standing too close, nigger. Get away from me. Nigger."

Or,

"What's the matter, boy? Somebody take your watermelon? Boy?"

The berating was nonstop with Newhart, and the other workers mostly stood by and watched—mouths open and amazed, but entertained nevertheless, like they were watching an improvisation troupe—anxious and excited about what might come out of his mouth next.

I started drinking a lot. Mostly to muffle the noise I was hearing every day at work, but at home, too. The neighborhood I lived in never seemed to sleep, and the night sounds became more and more menacing as clocks ticked toward day. I would need at least three beers to help me not hear the horns, sirens, souped-up engines, quarreling lovers, and barking dogs. I was always so confused by the barking. I never saw dogs during the day.

Workers at Northwestern—even the solitary Black guy—were allowed to take home dented cans and damaged cases of Michelob, Budweiser, Rolling Rock, and my favorite: Seagram's wine coolers. I was never without a surplus of sleep aid. Two or three drinks turned into six or eight very quickly, and what used to be an initiator of rest became a motivator for going out to bars and dance clubs.

* * *

I met Marylin after an Elks Lodge party turned wild and partygoers were forced into the streets to continue drinking, smoking, and searching for the next place to go. It was about three o'clock in the morning and no one was seeing straight, but Marylin looked directly at me and wouldn't blink. I looked away and then back again and she was *still* staring. She was frighteningly confident and forward as she walked over to me and grabbed my hand. "I'm Marylin," she said, never looking away, "and you're Louie."

Aside from an occasional pick-up game at The Phillips, I hadn't been called Louie since before leaving for Alpena. I couldn't believe this girl—this woman—knew who I was.

Maybe we went to high school together?

Maybe she was an old friend of Toni's?

Maybe one of my old teammates is playing a trick on me?

"I've heard about you," she said. "You were a couple of years behind me at Union. I've also heard that you are shy," she smiled. "That's okay … I'm not."

We were married three months later. There was no courtship. No getting to know one another. After twelve to fourteen hours of loading trucks each day, I would meet Marylin wherever she found herself that night, and I would buy her drinks. I suppose that was enough commitment for her to know that we should be married. I believed her. We didn't even say "I love you" until long after we spoke our vows. I did love her, though. At least I thought so. I was desperate for her approval. I longed to see her smile. Any amount of affection from her would send me over the moon. I would have done anything she ever asked of me. And I did.

Is that love?

At first, Marylin filled a great void. I didn't know what I wanted. So, she told me. I didn't have a plan. So, she made one for me. When I couldn't find words, she would speak for me. When I would complain about my job or about discrimination by Newhart, she would grab me by my face or twist a handful of my shirt and demand, "You be a man, Alton. Don't you dare let them treat you that way."

She wasn't wrong to get angry with me. I was not a good man. I wasn't even a good person. I drank too much, cursed too much, yelled too much, and ran away every time things got difficult. Slamming the door behind me, I'd turn on the stereo— Too $hort, ICE-T, N.W.A., or Boogie Down Productions—as loud as the speakers could go and scream the profanity-laced lyrics at her through the door.

No wonder she never respected me. No wonder she wanted out.

* * *

Meanwhile, the Teamsters strike meant more and better opportunities for me. Northwestern Beer was desperate for distribution drivers, so I made the jump—in responsibilities and pay—and started delivering beer all over Grand Rapids. I found out quickly that Newhart wasn't the only white person in Grand Rapids who had a problem with a Black guy working at Northwestern. Day after day, I was met with angry restaurant owners, bartenders, convenience store workers, and grocery store shoppers; all indignant that a Black man was in their presence.

An elderly lady stopped me in the aisle of a D&W Fresh Market and started rubbing my forearm. "I just wanted to see if I could get the black off," she said and then kept walking. "You're out of luck!" she called over her shoulder, laughing.

A manager at a 7-Eleven rushed through a line of patrons and stopped me at the front door. "Deliveries need to be made at the back, you idiot." As I apologized and said, "Yes, sir," he shot back, "That's right, nigger. You call me sir."

A policeman pulled me over on Interstate 96 because he thought I had stolen the Budweiser truck I was driving. After fifteen minutes of interrogation, he allowed me to make my delivery, but warned that I should "be careful being a Black guy around here."

I was delivering pallets of beer to a bar on the north end of Grand Rapids late one afternoon when a man at the bar turned and said, "Stop right there, nigger. Where the hell do you think you are?" I tried to explain that I was simply delivering beer that the bar had ordered, but he stood up with his hand behind his back and said, "I don't care if you're the nigger Santa Claus. If you take one more step into my bar, you're a dead man." Shaking and on the verge of tears, I went to the payphone across the street and called Jim Hoover to tell him what had happened. "Damn it, Alton. It's always something with you. Why did I hire a Black guy, anyway?" Thirty minutes later, a white driver from Northwestern showed up to take the dolly of beer inside the bar.

When I returned the truck at night, Newhart and his friends would be waiting to give me grief.

One night, a group of men approached the truck. "Where have you been, nigger?" Newhart stood at the garage door and called out again: "I asked you a question, boy. Where have you been, boy?"

I was exhausted. "I don't have time for this tonight, Newhart." I pushed past him and tried to make my way into the warehouse.

"Oh, you're gonna make time, boy. I'm tired of you. We're going to settle this tonight. Me and you. Man to monkey."

I stopped my stride and turned around. "What do you want from me, Newhart? What did I ever do to you?" My voice was trembling and I was about to cry.

"I don't like you, nigger. And I don't want you around here no more. Are you going to fight me, or am I going to just have to kill you where you stand?"

That was it for me. I had been battling panic attacks for weeks. I was constantly anxious and on the verge of breaking down. In the warehouse, in my truck, making deliveries, and especially at home.

Marylin had pulled away almost completely. I couldn't blame her, really. I was a shell of myself. We never talked or spent time together, and when we did find ourselves in the same room for more than a few minutes, she would end up berating me and blaming me for everything wrong in her life.

Including, now, the fact that she was pregnant.

I was about to be a father?

I agreed to meet Newhart a few blocks from the warehouse in a gas station parking lot. I knew I couldn't beat him in a fight, but I also knew I couldn't keep suppressing the hurt and anger and fear I had been carrying for what seemed like my entire life. And maybe, just maybe, fighting him would make me feel more like a man. More like a man about to be a father.

He brought his friends to watch. About twelve men—some I knew from the warehouse—gathered around as Newhart rushed toward me. I was faster than him. He was stronger than me. We circled the parking lot over and over. He flailed like a man on fire, and I was able to dodge his punches and kicks. "Stop running, nigger! Stop running away and fight me!" He was out of his mind. If he caught me, he would surely kill me. Suddenly, he stopped chasing me. I darted my head in every direction, making sure the others were not descending to block me in their ring of hate. We were both breathing heavily. A thin line of bright red streamed down Newhart's forehead. I must have scratched him trying to protect myself. I never threw a punch. Bringing his hand up to meet the blood, he looked at his fingers and then started laughing: "You gone and did it now, nigger."

He stood up straight and then started walking, slowly, backward toward his pick-up truck. Reaching into its bed, he pulled out a set of snow chains and let them dangle next to his right leg before charging toward me and screaming. He swung the chains over his head and then quickly down like he was wielding a whip. He swung high and I went low. He swung low and I jumped over it. I ran to my car and hid behind it as Newhart became winded and dropped the chains on the ground at his feet.

His posse encouraged him to let me go: He's *not worth it; you'll get him soon; tonight's not the night; come on, Newhart. Let him go.* They all stared at me as I inched around my car and got in the driver's seat. I was weeping as I drove away.

The next morning, Newhart chased me all the way to Jim Hoover's office where I begged our boss to make him stop harassing me. I told him what happened the night before and he laughed. "My god, Hardy. Why do you always have to cause so much trouble?"

He promised to call off Newhart and his boys while we were on Northwestern property, but that I should probably watch my back everywhere else. The best thing I had going for me there was the fact that Newhart would never dare follow me to "the Black part of town."

1990

∗ ∗ ∗

My marriage was miserable. There was no joy in our lives. Even the thought of a child of my own brought nothing but dread. My own experience with fatherlessness weighed heavily. I didn't want to be like my father, but I didn't know how to stop it. *Was this how my life was going to be? Is this what I have been living for?* The fear and loneliness I had endured for my twenty-four years on earth was slowly turning to bitterness and anger. I was pushing everybody out of my life. I never saw my old friends; I hardly spoke to Lucille. When she would reach out, I usually found an excuse or a work obligation to keep me from engaging.

My "mom," who had shown me nothing but love, acceptance, and hope for a better life than I could imagine for myself. I didn't even call her to tell her that I had a son.

I would drive my routes and make my deliveries every day, but I was never fully present. I felt like a witness to my actions, not a participant in them. I was tired all the time, but it wasn't physical fatigue as much as I was like a tangled sail, refusing to unfurl and catch wind. I stopped hearing the rude, vulgar, or racially offensive comments made by white people. I stopped hearing anything, really. But, when callouses build around your heart, it makes even the soft and wonderful and lovely things fall away.

I didn't view Marylin's pregnancy as a blessing. It was a punishment. And I didn't see my baby boy as a miracle.

He was another mistake. Another failure that I had somehow already established.

I began listening to cassette tapes of Louis Farrakhan speaking about Black superiority and how the white race was a created race, an inferior race, an underdeveloped race that hasn't evolved yet. "That's why they are angry! That's why they hate us," he would bellow and then whisper, "We as Black people have to be concerned about preparing a future for our people … Separation is the ultimate answer … and we must build up an army of righteousness." Farrakhan was putting my experience into language that I could understand. His anger was justified, and so I felt justified in mine. Better yet, he could voice his frustrations eloquently and with conviction, so I didn't have to.

We named our son Amaad Rashad Hardy. His name means "admirable one led to truth" in Arabic, but I didn't really care about that. I simply wanted to rebel against anything that might be considered under the influence of white America. To my knowledge, there aren't a lot of white "Amaad's" out there. Not in Grand Rapids, anyway.

Marylin didn't love me. She didn't even like me. She had no respect for me, and she let her feelings be known every chance she got. "You don't know how to do anything," she'd scream as I tried to secure Amaad's diaper or hold his bottle to his mouth.

"You're not holding him right. What are you trying to do, break his neck?" She hardly allowed me to hold the baby, and she would recoil and exhale in disgust if I ever tried to touch her. "I thought you were a real man," she repeated over and over, "but you are worthless. Why don't you just leave?"

Marylin consistently invited me to leave her and the baby for good. "We don't need you," she'd say. "We would be better off without you here. I don't love you, and neither will *he*."

Her words punctured my soul like a thousand tiny daggers, causing every ounce of self-love, self-worth, or will to seep out—drop by excruciating drop—until I believed her.

And then I got fired.

I had been on the clock for fourteen hours when I made a sharp right turn out of a convenience store and clipped the side of the canopy that covered the fuel pumps. The damage was minimal—just a small scrape along the very top of the trailer—but it was enough to convince Jim Hoover that I was more of a liability than a faithful employee. "I can get a warm body to fill your seat on just about any street corner from here to Detroit, Hardy. That's the last straw. You're fired."

I pleaded with him not to let me go. I even promised to pay for the damage out of my own pocket, but he wasn't having it. "That's what insurance is for. You think I'd let you idiots out there with my trucks without insurance?"

I imagined the look of achievement and pride on Newhart's face when he heard the news.

When Marylin found out, she almost lost her mind. And after thirty minutes of constant screaming, I finally lost mine. I stormed out of the house and drove away. I didn't have a destination in mind; I just drove. After stopping at the liquor store for two six-packs of Seagram's, I found myself on the banks of the Grand River near Riverside Park.

> *I bet it's deep enough.*
> *I could just drive right into it.*
> *Maybe I could jump from that bridge.*

The thought of killing myself, ending the misery, stopping the loneliness, removing myself from a world that clearly had no use for me, was nothing new. I had considered suicide many times over the years, but that night was different. Death seemed necessary. It seemed possible. I drank as much as I could as quickly as I could, and I continued to contemplate the best way to exit the shattered life I couldn't piece back together. And then, mercifully, I cried myself to sleep.

*　*　*

The weeks that followed are a blur. I spent my mornings drinking and my afternoons looking for odd jobs that could bring in a few dollars a day for food and beer. One day, after unsuccessfully finding work, I passed a familiar face on the sidewalk.

Was that Bobby?

From Union?

Is he wearing a suit?

Bobby Springer was two years older than me, so I never spent time with him in high school, but he was a local celebrity. One of the best basketball players to ever play for the Red Hawks. An injury his senior year kept him from playing college ball, but legends told of his talent on the court, and the legends were proved true every time I saw him pick up a ball at The Phillips. I knew of him, but I never considered him to be a friend. An idol, maybe, but we did not have a friendly relationship.

"Alton? Is that you, my brother?" Bobby beamed and flashed his perfect, white teeth as he turned around quickly and grabbed my arm. "Well, if it isn't Louisville, right here in the flesh! How are you, brother?" He called me "brother" twice in the span of ten seconds. I nervously returned his smile and responded, "Hey, Bobby. H-h-h-ow are you?"

After a few niceties and small talk that included him telling me about his beautiful wife, two amazing kids, and his job as a household items salesman, he said that I should bring Marylin and Amaad to visit his church. "It's a small gathering every Sunday, but I think you'd really like it," he said. "We're always looking for young families to come and grow with us."

He called me brother a few more times and then continued on, happily, to wherever he needed to be. When I got home, I told Marylin about seeing Bobby and being invited to Family Worship Center the next week.

"You don't need a church, Alton. You need a job. I'm pregnant again, you idiot."

I couldn't remember the last time she and I had been together. Surely, I was in a drunken stupor at the time, but the idea that we would ever have another child would not and could not have ever crossed my mind.

"Don't look so shocked," she said. "You shouldn't be surprised that you messed that up, too."

A few days later, I got a job. It was at a dairy company, and I was asked to do many of the same things I had done when I started at Northwestern Beer. I was loading and unloading trucks, helping to organize and move around products in the warehouse, and attacking any and every odd job that presented itself. The pay was noticeably less than I was used to, but the promise of promotion was clear, and for the most part, my bosses were fair and kind. After a few weeks of fourteen- to eighteen-hour days, their promises proved true and I was given a two-dollar and fifty-cent raise. I thought this accomplishment would come with great praise from Marylin, but the opposite was true. "Do you really think you can lead this family on $11.50 an hour? Grow up, Alton."

Over and over, I was met with rejection from the one person from whom I craved approval, but she made it clear that she would never give that to me. She would never respect, love, or be proud of anything I could give. The thought of bringing another child into our chaos was almost more than I could handle.

It was a Thursday afternoon as I was exiting a gas station market and carrying a twelve-pack of Miller High Life when I saw Bobby putting gas in his car. He smiled, big, and waved: "Louie, my brother! I was just thinking about you! What are you doing this Sunday? I'd love for you and your family to be our guests at FWCC!"

The Family Worship Center Church was having a revival of sorts that weekend, and Bobby promised "an exciting worship experience" if we could meet him there that morning. I told him that I wasn't sure if we could make it, but I appreciated the invitation. "Come see us, Louisville. It'll be good for your soul, brother." With that, he got into his pristine Oldsmobile Cutlass and drove away. I remember thinking that he seemed like the happiest person I had ever met—always smiling, always glad to see whoever might be in front of him.

I bet his wife is proud of him, I thought.

Saturday was a particularly long day at the warehouse. When I got home, Amaad was crying on the couch next to Marylin who never looked away from the TV. I leaned over and kissed my son on top of the head and tried to put my hand on Marylin's shoulder, but she shied away and huffed: "He's tired," she said. "Put him to bed."

After securing Amaad in his crib, I walked past my wife without saying a word and drove to a bar. I drank four beers before paying and walking out. An hour later, I was back, ordering another round and drinking them as fast as I could. I continued this routine at least four more times. When I wasn't at the bar, I was walking and talking out loud to a god who wasn't there. I was crying out loud and cursing the father who abandoned me, the mother who left me, the bosses who belittled me, and the wife who never loved me. I drank and wept and called out for help that simply was not coming. As drunk as I was, I was also strangely lucid. Every darkness I had ever encountered was coming fully to light. I prayed for the first time in years:

God, take me out of here.

* * *

Somehow, I was sober enough the next morning to drive to FWCC. I don't remember making the decision to go, but I suddenly found myself driving up and down the street looking for a place to park. This was a community church, nestled in a neighborhood off of a side street that met another two-lane road lined with old, poorly kept homes. There was no parking lot, and not an inch of curb that wasn't already being covered by rows and rows of vehicles—probably a half-mile long. I was sweating and felt sick to my stomach when I saw Bobby standing out front with his wife and kids. He was overjoyed to welcome his *brother* to this special place.

As we entered the tiny space, completely packed to the walls with people, I felt an overwhelming sense of belonging. Each face that I saw was smiling. Every eye that met mine was beaming with acceptance and welcome. Nothing specifically memorable happened to me that day, but I couldn't stop weeping. For over an hour, I had to be held up by Bobby and others as the weight of my entire life fell upon me and crumbled at my feet. It was supernatural.

I had been loved before that morning at Family Worship Center, but I don't think I had ever *felt* love in that way.

I went home a changed man. No more anger. No more anxiety. No more feeling lost and alone. No more inadequacy. I was different, and surely Marylin would see and feel the difference in me. Surely we would be able to reconcile and become whole.

But that's not how it worked.

My excitement about God and studying His Word was met with eye rolls and sarcasm. My longing to be with God's people at the church and for her and Amaad to join me was disregarded as ridiculous, or ignored altogether. She seemed to hate what was happening to me. For our entire relationship, she had been antagonizing me and chastising me for not taking control and being a man, and now that I had finally found something I believed in, something that was making me better, stronger, and more fulfilled, she turned her back. When she would let me take Amaad to church, she would go to bingo halls or clubs.

I prayed for her constantly. I prayed for our marriage. I tried putting into practice the lessons and learning that I was experiencing at FWC, but God did not seem to hear those prayers. The church was asking men to step up and take control of their houses and communities; to be leaders in prayer and in deed. They were calling us to become leaders, not just outside of the church walls, but inside as well.

My day-to-day at the dairy company was getting busier and more time-consuming with every month. I was working seven days a week, twelve- to fourteen-hour days, and spending less time than ever at home. Plus, I wasn't getting to go to church every Sunday, and that broke my heart. I thought it was time for a change. *How could I fully invest in my family and become a leader within my church if I was working all the time?*

The news that I had quit my job was not welcomed warmly by Marylin, and when I explained my reasons to her, she let out the most genuine laugh I had ever known her to muster. "You think you are going to be a leader? A pastor?" She was hysterical at this point. "You can't even talk right! Ain't nobody ever gonna listen to you!"

There are a few words and phrases that have been directed at me throughout my lifetime to which I have had a visceral response—but there is nothing that Marylin could have said in that moment that could have hurt any deeper than that. My whole body ached for weeks.

* * *

We welcomed our second child, Jalen, and things started to settle down a bit at home. Marylin and I were still at odds more often than not, but she seemed to soften a little, even allowing me to name our daughter. Perhaps she didn't have the strength to fight with me about it, but when I suggested we name her after my favorite basketball player, she didn't bristle at the idea.

Actually, Jalen Rose was one of my *five* favorite basketball players at the time—the entire starting roster for the Michigan Wolverines. The players were dubbed "The Fab Five" in the media and were possibly the greatest collection of collegiate players to ever grace a court at the same time. The other four players were Chris Weber, Juwan Howard, Jimmy King, and Ray Jackson. To me, the name "Jalen" was the only name that could go both ways—like a homonym, but with people.

Jalen was pure light. Smiling from the day she was born—a much easier baby to deal with than her brother. But Amaad was growing and starting to become a remarkable little boy. My love for those kids was true and deep.

Meanwhile, I had secured a new job—not a better job, per se, but a better job for our family and for my desire to spend Sundays at church. I worked the night shift at Parcel Corporation of America, a company that produced, sold, and shipped corrugated packaging. In other words, I stacked boxes in boxes in boxes from 10 p.m. until 6 a.m., Monday through Friday.

I was only making $7.20 per hour but was promised at least $20 per hour if I could get unionized. "That might take a couple of years," they told me, "but it's good money if you can stick around."

That was all I needed to hear. I worked harder and faster than I ever had at Northwestern or the dairy company. I had a purpose and drive like I had never known. I continued to be mesmerized by God and His people. Church was becoming the only place I wanted to be. I was memorizing Scripture, connecting with other members, and starting to believe that maybe God had a plan for my life.

On my sixtieth day at PCA, as I was folding the enormous stack of flat, cardboard boxes in front of me, I was approached by a supervisor that I had never met. "Grab your things," he grunted. "It's time for you to go." I was surprised and confused.

"E-e-excuse me, s-s-sir?"

"You heard me, nigger. Get your things."

My heart sank as his words echoed in my head, and all other sounds went silent. I couldn't hear the production chambers grinding, hissing, and pushing out sheets. I couldn't hear the printers or cutters or the voices of others working through the night. I was frozen. The supervisor doubled back and got in my face, threatening to call security if I didn't follow him to the office.

When we arrived to his makeshift perch above the production floor, he slammed the door to his closet-sized office and began sneering at me: "I'm so sick of you dumb niggers, I can hardly stand it! If I could fire every one of your black asses, I'd do it right now! I see you looking at me like you belong here, but by god …" he was screaming now, "by god, I'd sooner blow up this whole building with you in it than work another minute with your filthy, black ass!"

"I don't u-u-understand, sir. I think there's been some kind of m-m-mistake." I was in shock. Not just by what he was saying, but by the fact that he was saying it at all. The previous fifty-nine days had been flawless. Sure, there was a quick learning curve, but once I got the hang of the jobs ahead of me, I was accomplishing more than the next two guys combined.

I started to cry.

The supervisor got a few inches from my face and through clenched teeth said, "You're fired, nigger."

I backed away and ran out of the door to the office down the hall. It was John's office, the very place I had been hired just a few weeks before. I pleaded with him to explain what I had done. "I'll do better," I cried. "I'll do whatever you need me to do." John calmly backed his chair from behind his desk and stood up. "There's nothing I can do for you, son. If your supervisor says you gotta go … you gotta go."

The so-called supervisor followed me and closed the door behind him with his foot. I dropped to my knees and began weeping.

"Please don't do this. Please don't fire me. I've got a new baby. I need this job. Please don't do this."

Sandwiched between these two white men, I alternated my pleas back and forth as they just stared down at me. "I don't understand. Oh, God, please help me." I was screaming, begging for God to help me, and I think this angered the supervisor even more.

"You can pray all you want, but if I have to throw you out of here, you may never get up." His mouth was dripping saliva, like a boxer taunting his fallen opponent.

John stayed calm and crossed his arms. "Don't make us get security up here, boy. Come on. It's time to go home to them babies now."

By that time in my life, one might have assumed that I had already understood that hate doesn't need a reason. It doesn't necessarily grow because it has been fertilized by anything in particular. Hate doesn't need fertile ground from which to find its purchase. It just is, and it always will be, what it is.

I left PCA at 3:30 a.m. and sat, numb and silent, in my driveway until six. I could hear Marylin's voice in my head: *You're worthless. You are a failure. You can't even keep a job folding boxes.* It took every ounce of strength I could gather to make myself walk inside the house. Marylin would be getting ready for work. I had to tell her, and I was so broken that I wouldn't even be able to deny that I wasn't a real man. Even when I tried my hardest, I failed.

I made my way inside and found her in the bathroom, brushing her hair. The coos and grunts and morning squeals of our babies lightly filled the hallway as I fell to my knees at the door. I started crying, unable to catch my breath, but managed to say the words: *They. Let. Me. Go.*

Marylin rushed over to me and started pounding on my head with her hairbrush. She was wailing and screaming and calling me every name in her head. "How dare you come in here and tell me this! That's it, Alton! I'm done with you!" She was hitting me and screaming, and the babies began crying from the other room, and I was crying and begging her to stop.

I covered my head with my arms and inched impossibly closer to the floor, and then everything slowed down. I heard a clear, gentle voice tell me to get up.

"Get up, Alton. And stay up. This ends now. You will never be on your knees again, except for in worship of me. Get up."

* * *

Marylin kicked me out a few days later. For months, I tried to get back in her good graces, but that would be assuming I was ever there in the first place. Night after night—from the comfort of friends' couches, or the front seat of my car, I would make plans to try and win her back, to be able to be a father to my kids. But she had already moved on. I would sit in the parking lot of our old apartment building and watch as a different man, just about every night, would enter our apartment and then leave a few hours later. I sat there for hours, crying, praying, and asking God to redeem our marriage, to let me be the man that Marylin wanted and needed.

Once, I was sitting in my car when an elderly Black man approached my window. He tapped on the glass and asked me to roll the window down. I noticed him from seeing him around the complex. He was the repairman. I said hello.

"Son," he said, abruptly, "you gots to get up out of here. That woman ain't no good for you. Go on from this place …" He softened and said, "God's got something else planned for you, brother."

As he walked away, I struggled to find my breath. My body began shaking, and I let out a guttural scream like my life was being taken away. Maybe it was.

PART FOUR

SURELY THIS IS THE PROMISED LAND

Two months later, I stood in the back of my church as hundreds of people piled into the tiny room. It was a Sunday night, and a guest speaker was scheduled to deliver a special sermon. I had never heard David Ireland preach, but others raved about his particular style, which was to call people out of the congregation and tell them what God was saying to him … about them. Some called it the gift of prophecy, but I didn't know about all that.

The Right Reverend Ireland, as I had heard others refer to him, was a gifted communicator. He was loud when he needed to be, but also gentle as he preached on the sovereignty of God.

"He is all powerful, all knowing, all loving, and all good." There was a songlike cadence to his words. "He is divine, sublime; He is kind, and on time!" This guy was a performer! I had never seen anyone have fun from the pulpit, and his message brought a huge smile to my face.

His eyes met mine and he paused.

"Young man. Young man in the back. The tall one. Yes, you." He was pointing at me. "Come up here for a minute, my brother. Come on up. The Almighty has something he wants me to say."

I wanted to run. I wanted to trample over anyone in my way, press through those double doors, and disappear into the night.

The people around me started to clap and encourage me to go. A few "amens" and "alleluias" rang out as I stepped forward and ever so slowly made the walk up to the front of the church. It was only a few steps, but it seemed like a mile long. I was shaking.

Reverend Ireland put his hand on my shoulder and addressed the congregation: "Does anybody here know this young man? What's his name?"

"Alton!" someone shouted from the back.

"Louie!" Laughter sprinkled throughout the church as Bobby peeked his head around the person in front of him and flashed those great, big, smiling eyes.

"Brother Alton. Brother Louie." Ireland got very quiet.

"You and your family have experienced great tragedy. Racism has darkened your door more times than most. You have been mistreated, hated, and despised because of the color of your skin."

Adrenaline rushed through my body like hot grease, and I turned to meet his eyes. He was crying.

"Because of your pigmentation and eth-ni-ci-ty"—the enunciation of the word "ethnicity" was jarring, almost sarcastic—but he didn't leave room for questions. He continued: "You have been burdened, my brother. More so than most, because God is telling me that you are a reconciler. In your heart, you want to forgive the atrocities that have kept you angry, scared, and alone. You want peace, my brother, and it is peace that you will find."

The room exploded with applause, but he let go of my shoulder and motioned for the crowd to quiet. "Hear me, though, brother. Listen close. These people who have burdened you with their hate will learn to love you and you will learn to love them. You will win them over, but not because of what you can do. Peace will come from God. Through Jesus. The Prince of Peace. He will use you to bring about what your heart desires."

With that, the room erupted again, and the people stood and clapped and sang "amen and amen," and I was asked to return to my place in the back.

As I stood there, trying to take in all that had just happened, a sense of calm came over me, and I thought to myself:

This dude is crazy.

I would be lying if I said I didn't think about the Right Reverend's prophecy over the coming days and weeks, but I kept reminding myself:

You are a jobless, homeless, directionless, weak-as-water, stuttering fool who can't keep a job, a wife, a roof over your head, or a bottle out of your hand. God's not going to use you to reconcile nothing but where your next meal comes from ...

I wanted to do right, live right, make good decisions, and become a better man. I just still didn't know how. My divorce was final, and I was devastated. I knew Marylin wasn't right for me. I knew I wasn't right for her. I knew that I could never measure up to all she had once hoped for or needed, but I just didn't want to fail. I ventured in and out of depression and self-loathing. I wasn't going out and carousing like I used to, but I still had to drink wine coolers every night to fall asleep.

Throughout even the darkest days, I was still worshipping God. That was the only thing in my life I felt worthy of—literally and figuratively falling on my face every chance I got—to beg for and then feel the love and acceptance I couldn't find anywhere else.

* * *

Deion, a friend I had met through church, had a two-bedroom apartment and found himself living alone after he found his wife sleeping with the next-door neighbor. Deion was supposed to be at work that Saturday morning, but decided to take the day off and surprise his bride of only six weeks with a bagful of doughnuts.

He was looking for a roommate by that afternoon.

I couldn't pay Deion to live in his second bedroom, but he agreed to let me stay there for a few weeks. I was working at Martin Luther King Park on the outskirts of Madison, near Ottawa Hills. My job consisted of walking around, picking up trash, smiling at happy families enjoying the jungle gyms, and making sure the gates were locked before the sun disappeared beyond the Grand Rapids skyline. I was twenty-eight years old, making $6 per hour, and the most important thing I did every day was lock a gate that could be easily stepped over by most anyone over the age of nine.

That gate was a popular hangout for other city and park employees. Often, I had to shoo away married men and their girlfriends from the park exit. I never caught anyone having relations back there, but there was *a lot* of kissing.

While I walked around the park, I would listen to preacher tapes on my Sony Walkman. Elders at the church would pass me a tape every now and then with sermons from Dr. Miles Monroe, Bishop T.D. Jakes, Frederick Sampson, or Gardner Calvin Taylor, and I would drink in their messages like water to a refugee.

One afternoon, I was listening and walking when I saw a group of people about my age. They were harmlessly hanging out, drinking beers, and causing no trouble at all, but drinking wasn't allowed on park property. I decided to keep walking, finish the sermon, and circle back. If they were still there when I returned, I'd stop and say something.

Fifteen minutes later, I approached the group and asked them to please throw away their bottles and leave the park. There were a few grumbles from the crowd and a few more choice words thrown my way, but then a girl stood up, smiled at me, and told her friends to be quiet.

"He's just doing his job, y'all. Come on. Let's go." She smiled again and then helped usher the others out to the parking lot. As they disappeared behind the gate, I realized that I was still smiling. I exhaled and then heard the words: *That woman is going to be your wife.* I was shocked out of my daze and then realized that I was still wearing my headphones.

I must have heard that wrong.

* * *

The next few weeks at church were horrible. The lead pastor at Family Worship Center had been having an affair for quite some time, so the elders approached him and asked him to step down. He refused, and also refused to admit his wrongdoing. Many people left the church, and those of us who stayed grieved the animosity and heartache that this split had caused.

One of my mentors, a man named Arthur Bailey, was a gifted and faithful man of God, and decided to break away from FWC and start his own church. I prayed for God to direct me and show me what I should do, and my decision became abundantly clear as I heard Arthur address a tiny gathering of followers the next week. After a short welcome, he opened the floor to anyone who might feel led to pray God's blessings on that group. Before I could talk myself out of speaking, I began to pray out loud. For the first time in my life, I was beseeching God on behalf of others, in front of others.

I stumbled my way through the few minutes I allowed myself to pray, but when I spoke "amen," I raised my eyes to see that the others were crying. I don't know what I said. I don't even know how I said it, but that prayer helped everyone there know that Arthur's leadership, and his new "Abundant Life Church," would help us all grow closer to God and begin to reveal the plan He had for our lives.

For the next year and a half, Abundant Life met on Sunday afternoons at various locations in and around Grand Rapids, and I continued to grow in my faith. Arthur often invited me to open or close our meetings in prayer, and I grew more and more comfortable talking to God in front of others.

I was still staying at Deion's apartment, still unable to pay him for my room, and still making $6 per hour at the park when he came to me and said that he couldn't afford to live there anymore. He had decided to move in with his mother, across town, so he could save some money and try to get back on his feet. Before I could panic, he said that he had told his mother about me and that she had agreed to let me stay there, too. A kindness I had only experienced one other time in my life. Deion's mother was a carbon copy of my mom, Lucille Carlisle, who was still housing her *entire* family tree all those years later.

I moved in with Deion's mother and was given the entire basement, complete with a full bathroom and a tiny kitchen. Aside from the dampness in the air and an occasional leaky pipe overhead, it was the nicest place I had ever stayed.

I finally had a suitable environment for visits with Amaad and Jalen, and looked forward to every opportunity Marylin would allow me to see them. I loved spending time with my kids. It broke my heart to watch them leave, but the thought of them coming back for visits would usually sustain me for a couple of weeks.

Seeing them, though, would remind me that I was still alone. I was still longing for something I could not see or feel or understand.

I still couldn't sleep at night, because my mind would constantly race with memories, both happy and painful. Many were both.

All of them were without a father.

From time to time, Marylin would allow the kids to stay the night with me in the basement. I found myself watching them sleep and mourning the loss I felt deep in my soul. One night, I sat, looking at my sleeping kids—so innocent, so small—and I began weeping.

What will become of these children?

How will they ever know the depth of my love for them?

How can I ever convince them that I will always love them? No matter what!

Then, as if He had walked into the room and sat with me on the bed, I heard God speak to me:

Look at your children, Alton. Feel the love you have in your heart. Take in the details of their faces, their hands and feet, the hair on their head. These are YOUR children, Alton. You are their father. And I am yours.

I fell on my knees and I prayed. I had never thought of God as Father. I had never fully understood the Abba Father of the Bible. I had never claimed Him as anything other than a Power to be feared and revered. But in that moment, our relationship changed. My longing subsided and was replaced with a longing to know Him more. To believe His promise to love me. Always. No matter what. He is the Father I have always needed. I am the child He always wanted.

Then, I fell asleep and truly rested. Maybe for the first time in my life.

* * *

The next day, after breakfast, I ran out to my car to retrieve a stuffed animal that Jalen had left the night before. I was shirtless, shoeless, and wearing only an old pair of basketball shorts.

It'll be a quick jaunt, there and back, I thought. *Surely no one will see me.*

After grabbing the stuffed animal, I slammed the door and began bouncing from my right foot to my left, trying to dodge felled acorns and other debris. Then, I looked up to see a girl out of the corner of my eye. I sprinted behind a tree. I must have looked like a baby giraffe learning to run on its own; so skinny, awkward, and uncoordinated.

Wait.
Do I know her?
Who is that?
I know that smile.
She's beautiful.
I've seen her befo …

It was the girl from the park. The girl who smiled at me … two years ago! "That woman is going to be your wife."

I recalled that entire scene as if it had happened the day before. I was shocked, but also immediately aware that I was standing half-naked on the sidewalk, holding a pink bunny rabbit. I squeezed my eyes, tight. *That's the girl from the park! Maybe she didn't see me. Of course she saw me!*

She didn't see me.

"That woman is going to be your wife."

The details—what she was wearing that day, how she stood up, that smile—were crystal clear. I peeked around the tree to see her happily bouncing up the stairs of the home across the street. As she disappeared behind the front door, I heard that voice again.

"Told ya," He said. "I keep my promises."

* * *

A few days later, we found ourselves outside at the same time and I gathered the courage to approach her. I lowered my head and raised my eyebrows as if to say, "Sorry about the half-naked, baby giraffe-thing," and she started laughing.

"I know you," I said. "I don't know your n-n-n-name, but I-I-I kn-now you."

"Is that right?" She smiled. "How do you know me?"

"It's not important," I said. "But I'd l-l-like to k-n-n-now you better." I smiled back.

* * *

Sandra. The most beautiful girl in the world. The most graceful person I had ever known. Like a sunrise that never set. She gave me life, immediately. And she took my breath away every day. I had never been in a dating situation—a courtship. I had never even seen one played out by others. But it wasn't a struggle with her. It was natural. It was comfortable. It was real. And she saw me—a boy trying so hard to become a man. Her smile was pure joy, which brought me to tears over and over again.

We spent every possible moment together. She also had two kids from a previous marriage, and we cherished the opportunities all four of our kids got to spend time and play together. My whole world fit within a three-mile radius of my basement apartment, but I was beginning to see something much bigger and better than the world around me. I had love that was deeper and broader than the ends of the earth. I realized that I had never been happy before. I had certainly experienced happy things, relationships, and circumstances, but this was more.

I've heard love described as a feeling, an emotion, an intangible idea that cannot be grasped. I disagree. Love is a living, breathing thing, and it takes many forms. Sandra was love, personified.

We were together for a year and a half before we got married. It was a very small ceremony performed by Arthur Bailey and his wife, Malvena. Our kids were there. My mom, Lucille, was there. A few friends, including Bobby Springer and his family, and some extended family on Sandra's side. That was it. A short, underwhelming ceremony that changed everything. Forever.

Sandra and I began going to church together every chance we got. Her heart was being softened and changed, too. We started reading the Bible and praying together. I also got a new job as a delivery driver and was able to create my own schedule, bid on specific jobs, and somewhat become my own boss.

Arthur preached a sermon one Sunday on the story of Joseph that he titled, "What Men Intended for Evil, God Used for Good." He said that sometimes, God allows bad things to happen to us; He allows discomfort, pain, loneliness, and other hardships to come our way so we might be better prepared for the journey ahead.

I didn't understand at first. What was I being prepared to do? As happy and contented as I was at that time, I felt like I was always playing catch-up. I hadn't gotten anywhere in life. I still felt like the six-year-old little boy looking up at the trees and searching for something, anything. The only place I felt fully present was in church, listening to the words of men tell the story of a God I so desperately wanted to understand. Most of my life had been lived in reaction to circumstances. How was I supposed to move toward God's will?

1997

* * *

Sandra gave me the gift of our son, Jeremiah, on a Thursday morning. Two weeks later, at a Saturday night church gathering, an elderly lady approached me to congratulate me. Before leaving, she said she had a word she wanted to share. She said that God had put it on her heart to tell me that He was going to pluck me out of where I was and put me in front of a new crowd and a new community that He was preparing for me and my family. And then she smiled and said, "And you are going to serve Him in new and extraordinary ways, young man!"

Her words reached me at a time when I was questioning just about every decision and movement I made. I was working, and it was good. But it wasn't enough. We had a new child. But how could I lead him and love him well? I had a wife whom I loved more than I ever thought I could. But how could I ever measure up? I had a relationship with God, my Father, but what was He calling me to do?

You are going to serve Him in new and extraordinary ways?

Arthur started giving me more and more responsibilities at Abundant Life. As one of the first few members of that church, I was a face and a presence that most people knew and expected to see every week. "I'd like for you to preach next Sunday," he said as he approached me casually, as if he was making a routine comment about the weather. I looked at him, puzzled, and then laughed the comment away. "I'm serious, Alton. I need you. God and His people need you. I'm thinking next Sunday is the time."

I almost blacked out. I tried to argue with Arthur, but he wasn't hearing it. "This is between you and God, now, my brother. I just do as I am told, and He told me it's time."

The next six and a half days were excruciating. I couldn't sleep. I couldn't eat. I couldn't even pray without getting distracted or bursting into tears. Sandra tried to calm my nerves and quiet the voices that were screaming, *You're not ready. You're not worthy. You can't even speak two sentences without stuttering and making a fool of yourself. This is going to be a disaster. This is going to ruin you. You are going to fail.*

Sunday morning, I spent just about every minute leading up to service time in the bathroom. I hadn't eaten a full meal in almost a week, but somehow I was still able to vomit more times than I could count.

As I made my way to the pulpit, my knees buckled and I almost fell out right there in front of everybody. It was packed. Either the church bulletin failed to mention that I would be giving the sermon, or everyone came out to watch the train wreck about to take place right there in the sanctuary.

I need you, Father. Give me the supernatural, Lord.

I preached on Matthew 14, the passage where Jesus walks on water. After introducing the text and asking everyone to stand so that I could read the text aloud, everything seemed to slow down. My heart stopped racing. My hands stopped shaking. My knees stopped knocking. And my stutter, for the first time in my life, went completely away.

Jesus approached the men in the boat. They were afraid. Storms were all around them. He was walking toward them on the water, and said,

*Sometimes we simply have to trust in the God who loves us and wants
the best for us in order for Him to do miraculous things with our lives.
Do you trust Him today? He's calling out to you right now:
Come to me.*

After the service, I was bombarded with people congratulating
me, commenting on how they were affected, deeply, by the words I
spoke. Sandra rushed to me and gave me a hug that lasted for what
felt like twenty minutes. And Arthur approached me, smiling, and
said, "Amen."

I wept for three days. At home. In my delivery truck. At the park
with Jeremiah. I couldn't stop weeping in complete awe of what
God had done. I wanted more. And I wanted *everyone* to feel what
I was feeling. I wanted to share what God was teaching me, with
people *like* me: struggling, weak, downtrodden, sinful, broken, and
hopeless people.

Like me.

Over the next several years, I was able to fill in for Arthur
when he was sick, traveling, or simply not able to preach. Every
experience I had in front of a congregation was Spirit-led and
Spirit-filled. God was teaching me and using me to share His hope
and promise with others.

Arthur was tired. He had been leading Abundant Life Church
for nearly a decade, and it was wearing him down. I felt like it might
be time to find another church family—a place that was excited to
preach the Word, and exciting to be a part of—but I was loyal to

Arthur and couldn't imagine leaving the man and the ministry who had done so much for me and my family.

Around this time, Sandra had taken a job with an inner-city ministry in downtown Grand Rapids, a place that served the underserved and helped down-and-out individuals and families get back on their feet. She was doing great work, for good, and meeting a lot of likeminded folks who wanted to help people that had grown up like I did—homeless, fatherless, poor, and alone.

One such kindred spirit was a worship minister at Madison Square Christian Reformed Church, the very same church that sat just a few hundred yards from Toni's old apartment on Madison Avenue.

"I've heard great things about your husband," she said one day as the two of them were packing lunches for a homeless shelter. "People say he is a gifted speaker." Sandra had to laugh at that comment, because she knew what a struggle it had been for me to speak in front of people. "Yes," Sandra replied. "God has been doing great things through Alton for several years. He's not a pastor, though. He just loves Jesus." The two of them laughed and went on about their work.

A few days later, the lady from Madison Square mentioned me again to Sandra: "I think your husband should come and talk to Pastor Dave. We're looking for someone like him to preach from time to time." Sandra made sure her new friend hadn't misunderstood their last conversation and told her, again, that her husband was not a pastor. "Alton is a delivery man. He has his own truck and delivers packages. He's not a pastor."

"Well, my friends used to go to Abundant Life," she responded, more seriously this time, "and they know your husband. I really think he needs to meet with Pastor Dave."

A week or so later, at Sandra's urging, I found myself sitting in Dave Beelan's office at the church I knew so well, but only from the outside. Pastor Dave, as he was affectionately known by everyone at the church, had been the lead pastor at Madison for almost twenty years when I met him. He was a vibrant, young-looking, but older white man who met me with a huge smile and a hug. "You must be Alton Hardy? I can't tell you how nice it is to meet you!"

I was overwhelmed. First of all, that was the first time a white person had ever hugged me. I was thirty-seven years old and had never been embraced by a person with skin that didn't look like mine. In fact, other than my wife, I couldn't recall ever being squeezed like that by another human being, Black or white.

I apologized for my clothes—I was still wearing my delivery uniform—and he waved me off like he was trying to get rid of a housefly. "Don't be ridiculous," he huffed, "if there's one thing you'll learn about me real quick, it's that I don't give two hoots what you look like!" He put me at ease immediately. I felt like I was sitting across from someone I had known for years. I could feel the tears pooling in my eyes, so I wiped them away as soon as he looked down at the papers on his desk.

"Let me tell you why you're here, friend."

For the next thirty minutes, Pastor Dave not only gave me a history of the church; he laid out their plan for the future: "We do ministry here on our spiritual gifts, Alton, which we believe are given to everyone by the Holy Spirit. That means we have all been created on purpose, for a purpose. God doesn't make any mistakes. We truly believe that. Do you believe that, Alton?"

I could only nod my head, *Yes*.

He continued: "We believe it takes all kinds of people to fulfill God's plans here on earth, and so that's why you're here this afternoon. I'd like to invite you to join us for the next few weeks, you and your family, of course, to let you see what we're all about. Maybe God will show you a few things while you're here."

I don't remember saying a word to the man. I had been asked to bring a few cassette recordings of messages that I had delivered over the years, so I left those with him, but I truly can't recall saying anything to him. I just forced a series of nods, smiles, a few throat clearing grunts, and a chuckle or two.

The next Sunday, Sandra and I joined Pastor Dave and a few others for lunch after church. Dave leaned over to me and told me that he had listened to the tapes. "You have a gift, Alton." He grabbed my hand. "I'd like for you to share that gift with us next Sunday in our evening service, if it's okay with you. It's not a large gathering, so you shouldn't feel overwhelmed by it. I just think our people will like to hear what you have to say."

It all happened so fast. I wasn't sure that I was ready, but I agreed. Sandra was a great encouragement throughout the next week, constantly building me up and telling me that God was in control. "You just do you, baby. God will take care of the rest."

I was praying that God would take the burden away from me and change Dave's mind, but that didn't happen. Sunday night came, and I preached the sermon on Matthew 14, asking the 300 people in attendance—most of them white:

Do you trust Him today? He's calling out to you right now:
Come to me.

Sandra was right. I just did what I knew to do, and God took care of the rest. The service was over, and Dave asked me to come back to his office. "Alton, how did you do that? Where did you learn to do that? Do you even know what you just did?" At first, I thought

I was in trouble. I must have had a concerned look on my face, because he burst out laughing and gave me a huge hug.

"Brother," he was smiling from ear to ear, "I could try for thirty years to teach people to deliver a sermon like you just did, and it would never happen. What you just did in that room cannot be taught. Brother, if you can stay humble and stay committed to God's Word, and if you continue to lean on Him for guidance every day, I am going to start with you what God is going to finish *through* you. You were created to preach His Word."

Created on purpose. For a purpose.

Little did I know, but Dave and his team had been working on a master plan for Madison Square that included bringing on three others to help create a Preaching Team at the church: a Black guy, a Hispanic guy, a woman, and himself. The job came with a salary, medical insurance, which I had never had, a 401(k), which I had never even heard of, and the responsibility of preaching every fourth Sunday.

Before taking on preaching duties, I was invited to take a few assessment tests: Old and New Testament History, Books of the Bible, Scripture Memorization, and a few others. I zeroed out on just about every one, but Dave stayed positive and said that the tests were just benchmarks to let me see where I could improve.

"There's no such thing as failing church," he laughed. "You got this."

I memorized the books of the Bible, in order, first. It took me about a week. Then, I committed to learning a new verse of Scripture every day. When I felt good about reciting the words, I tried to actually understand them. God was gentle with me throughout those first few weeks, but I was not very easy on myself. I was like a fighter in training: up before the sun, a healthy breakfast, and then off to train until I couldn't see straight. After a month of studying seven days a week, I certainly didn't know everything, but I knew enough to not "fail church."

Dave assigned me a passage to spend time with and asked me to apply it to my life and what I believed. He said to really spend time with the text and to pray about what God wanted me to see and hear in those words, "because that is what you'll be preaching on next Sunday morning," he said.

Sunday morning?
Not Sunday night?
Three thousand people show up on Sunday mornings!

"Are you sure?" I asked. "You want me to preach on Sunday *morning?*"
"You're a part of the Preaching Team, Alton. That's what we do."

Sunday, February 19, 2005

❋ ❋ ❋

The church was wall-to-wall with people. Standing room only. I had only seen that many people in the sanctuary one time before, and it was because we only had one service that day. This Sunday, we were having three! I assumed I was going to get off fairly easy that morning, because Grand Rapids was in the middle of a snowstorm. The flakes were as big as my hand and stacking up like bricks on sidewalks and bridges. *Surely there will only be a handful of people to show up*, I thought.

After the call to worship and morning hymn, Pastor Dave said a prayer and introduced me, for the first time, to Madison Square Christian Reformed Church.

As the applause waned, I began to pray:

"Father in heaven. I need you right now. Please use me, your servant, to speak the words you want spoken, to tell the story you want told, and to bring honor and glory to your name and your name only, Lord. Amen."

And then, silence. The entire congregation sat, completely silent and still, looking up at me as if I were about to announce lottery numbers. Most of the faces were white. Some of them were Black or Hispanic. But all of them were fixed on me. I stood there without moving or saying a word for a painfully long time. There was a cross near the back of the stage, a large, wooden cross, like a statue, affixed to the floor. I made my way slowly to it and leaned on it. This was not an act. I wasn't making a performative gesture. I genuinely thought I was going to fall down. I prayed, silently: *Help me, Jesus. Only You, Jesus.* And then I began to speak.

Pastor Dave had given me Ephesians 4:31 as my directive for that day, so I recited the words to the text: *Get rid of all bitterness, rage and anger, brawling and slander, along with every form of malice.* After pausing again to catch my breath, I began to tell my story. All of it.

Sardis. Selma. The snakes. Mama Fat. Walking alone. Eating from the dump. The hoppergrasses. The mud pies. The abuse. Watching my brother swing from a tree. My dobbage tags. The poverty. The fatherlessness. Louisville. Being spit on. Abandonment. Heart attacks. Hunger. Loneliness. Homelessness. Basketball. Attempted suicide. Failure. Alcohol. Nigger. Monkey. Nigger. On my knees. Failed marriage. Boy. Worthless. Nigger.

I think my eyes were closed the entire time I recalled the details of my life, because when I opened them, I saw that every single person in that sanctuary was weeping. I was crying, too, when I belted out the words:

"How can you not be bitter? How can we not be filled with anger and rage? How are we supposed to get rid of brawling and slander and every form of malice?"

The words echoed throughout the room that soon turned silent.

"Verse 32 tells us how: Forgiveness. *'Be kind and compassionate to one another, forgiving each other, just as in Christ, God forgave you.'* Forgiveness! Brothers and sisters, we can let go of our sins, because *we* are forgiven. Me and you and him and her and everyone. That is the Good News. *We are forgiven.*"

Something supernatural happened that morning. I fell on my knees and told God's story through my life, and hearts were changed, including mine. Right then and there. Right there in that room. The sanctuary erupted with applause and cheers like I had never heard. Men and women came to me and shook my hand. They thanked me for the words God gave me and continued weeping long after the service was over. Pastor Dave stood at the side of the stage and put his hand over his chest as if to say "thank you," and I returned the gesture.

His father, who must have been eighty years old at the time, approached me and said, "Son, you are a prophet of God. I hope you are ready. You are about to be used in a mighty way… on the level of Martin Luther King. I believe that. Thank you, sir. Thank you. Thank you."

Throughout the coming weeks, I battled with self-doubt and felt like an imposter time and time again as people continued to talk about and discuss the sermon I gave that day. But God was doing something in my soul, and He kept telling me to rest. Sandra's words kept echoing in my head: "You just do you, baby. God will take care of the rest." And He did.

Every fourth Sunday was another opportunity for me to use parts of my story to share the gospel. I was becoming known, even beyond the walls of Madison Square, as a reconciler. I preached about racism being the root of all evil—the sin of our age—but that we had a choice to make: *we can choose to keep being passionate about the sins of the past, or put our energies toward the Plan that God has for His people. And that begins with forgiveness.*

Later that year, I delivered a sermon from 1 Samuel, entitled, "Goliath and the Sin of Racism." The story is about David, a man after God's own heart, and Goliath, an unconquerable giant who represented all that was ungodly. David, of course, defeats the giant using limited resources and the Power of God Almighty. "How long are we gonna let Goliath punk us?" I cried out from the stage. "We are a generation right here and now that *must* be like David and do the will of God!"

In and among all of the truths that God was using me to communicate, a darkness started to creep in. Forgiveness started to become less of a message note, and anger started to grow in its place. Bringing back the stories of my childhood started to unearth pain that I thought was no longer a part of me.

August 16, 2006

* * *

My mama died. She had been admitted to an assisted living facility in Buffalo a few months earlier, and I never got a chance to go visit before she passed. Sandra and I took Jeremiah with us to the funeral. I thought it would be a great opportunity for my brothers and sisters to meet my wife and son, and I looked forward to showing them off. The funeral service was only about twenty minutes long, but that was an appropriate amount of time, given the slight gathering of fifteen or so mourners. I offered a prayer and thanked God for a mother who did her best with what she was given, and gave all that she had to the people she loved. It was a sincere prayer. I really did believe she tried her best.

After the service, Sandra and Jeremiah were talking and playing with Toni and others, so I gathered all the breath I could hold and walked over to sit with my father on a small bench looking out on Lake Huron.

I hadn't been in the presence of my father for almost thirty years. I couldn't recall the last time I had seen him, and I was sure he wouldn't remember me, his ninth-born child. The one who stuttered when he talked. The one who wet his pants until he was nine. The one who refused to walk. The one who was scared of his own shadow. The one who spent most of his time hiding from the father he never had.

I sat down next to him and exhaled.

"That was a fine prayer, son." He didn't look away from the water when he spoke. "She would have liked that," he said. A lump gathered in my throat as I turned and looked at the old, feeble man beside me. He was pencil-thin. His clothes hung on him like a bed sheet drying on a line. He shuffled behind a walker and had to be helped up and down when he needed to move. His eyes were yellowed and fading, and his hands shook slightly as he arranged the large hearing aid that dangled by his right cheek.

My heart ached for him somehow. This man who had brought nothing but pain and grief, sadness and bad memories to his family. I didn't feel anger about those things. I was just sad.

"Why did you treat her the way that you did?" The words escaped my lips before I could hold them. "Why did you hate Mama?"

He turned to look at me for the first time. "Oh, I didn't hate your Mama, boy. I didn't hate your Mama." A tear rolled down his cheek. I was certain this was the first time he had ever cried in his seventy-seven years on earth. Then another fell. And another.

"What you said about her was true. She did the best she could. But so did I, Alton."

He knew who I was.

"I didn't have no hope," he said. "I didn't have nothin' at all." He paused for a long time and then looked back to the lake.

"Neither did you. Or Eddie. Or Frank. Or Russell. Or Doris." His breath staggered as he listed every one of his kids by name. "Or Donald, Ronald, Toni, Andre, Vernon, Charles, or Niles. None of y'all had nothing." His voice cracked, and more tears fell. "And I couldn't give it to you."

"I just lost hope, son. I just lost hope. I just lost hope." He said it over and over until we both broke down and cried together. I leaned over, with my elbows on my knees, and he put his hand on my head. I didn't want that moment to ever end.

After a few more minutes, Sandra brought Jeremiah over to shake his grandfather's hand, and then I helped my father to the car that was waiting to take him to Mama's graveside.

I never saw him again.

That experience—those few moments with my father and seeing the brokenness and shame that enwrapped his body—brought a sadness I had never known. I was broken and didn't know how to ease the pain I was feeling. I was a leader in a church whose message was based on reconciliation and letting go of bitterness, but I had just seen a man, my father, who had endured and was still enduring the deepest darkness most couldn't imagine in their most vicious nightmares.

How can this be reconciled?

I didn't want to talk about race anymore. I was beginning to believe that Goliath was bigger than I thought. I didn't want to think about whites and Blacks and reconciliation and forgiveness. This was too much. It was bigger than my pulpit, and more than I could handle. I prayed to God for weeks and weeks: "Dear God, please don't make me do this no more. Please don't make me do this. It's too much. I love you, God, and I want to be your servant, but I can't do this no more. Please, Lord. No more."

* * *

But He didn't let me off the hook. "Goliath is big, Alton," He said. "But I am bigger. I Am."

Through many sleepless nights and lots of prayer, time in His Word, and time with my family, God, the Father, was reminding me that there is hope, and that I had an opportunity to help bring that hope to people like me—like my earthly father. He reminded me that there is room for pain and sorrow on this side of heaven, but that He is not a part of regret. God deals in relationships and healing. God deals in restoration, and it is the gospel that restores.

Day after day, my time with God was revealing more about His plan for His people: *That we might lean fully on Him and begin to understand, live out, and share the mercy and grace He pours into us with every breath.*

And then, standing in my bedroom one morning, I fell to my knees as I read John, chapter 17, verses 20 through 23. In the chapter, Jesus prays aloud in front of His disciples as He is preparing Himself and His friends for His impending death. First, He prays to be glorified, then He prays for their protection, and then He prays for the rest of the world: *that all of them may be one, Father, just as you are in me and I am in you … so that they may be brought to complete unity.*

Jesus' final hope for His children was that we be brought to complete unity?

I fell on my face and thanked God for His Word. I thanked Him for His Son. And I thanked Him for not giving up on me. My eyes, full of tears, had never seen more clearly. This was not about racism. It was about the restoration of souls.

How can we, as a people, as children of the living God, learn to live together?

To unify.

Understanding my internal struggle over the past several weeks and months, Pastor Dave came to me and said that he wasn't going to give me the passage for my next sermon. "Preach on whatever you want," he smiled and squeezed my shoulder. "Whatever the Lord puts on your heart."

Thank goodness, I thought. *I don't have to preach on Ephesians. I don't have to preach about race.*

Then, as I was sitting alone in my room, on my bed, trying to determine the message I wanted to share, I closed my eyes and opened my Bible. Ephesians.

Good grief.

Chapter 3. Verse 10: *Now, through the church, the manifold wisdom of God should be made known to the rulers and the authorities in the heavenly realms.*

The manifold wisdom of God? What does that mean?

The word "manifold," translated, means "many and varied; having many features and forms; wrought in various colors; diversified, intricate, complex, many-sided." God's wisdom in His extraordinary plan for His people is a multi-faceted, many-colored, culturally diverse, rich, and beautiful community of believers.

Good grief, indeed.

As I explained this verse and this idea that God miraculously showed me in the quiet of my room, I became more and more excited about the charge I had been given so many years before. As I stood in the back of the Family Worship Center, and Reverend Ireland encouraged me: "In your heart, you want to forgive the atrocities that have kept you angry, scared, and alone. You want peace, my brother, and it is peace that you will find … These people who have burdened you with their hate will learn to love you and you will learn to love them. You will win them over, but not because of what you can do. Peace will come from God. Through Jesus. The Prince of Peace. He will use you to bring about what your heart desires."

The threads of the world, woven together, to create the masterpiece that God has created with and through us.

All of us.

Together.

2008

* * *

As I was beginning to preach more about reconciliation, I was learning to understand the gospel. I started speaking and teaching about the purpose of the Church and the intended makeup of the family unit. Those are crucial to the Plan God has for His people. I really believe and believed that. But that's a tough message to convey to people—especially in an urban setting.

The inner city is a hopeless place. When people are quite literally dying in the streets, begging for their next meal, or doing unimaginable things just to make it to the next sunrise, they are not looking for answers. They need relief. The flip side is the fact that those who have what they need don't want to be told how to live; they simply want to know where to give.

I started being met after my sermons with comments like, "Pastor, it's just not going to change this side of heaven," so I would address those comments during my next sermon:

"That's bull!" I'd scream. "It's simply not true! Ephesians doesn't say 'when we get to heaven.' The Word of God states very clearly, 'Here. On this side of heaven!' And I'm not saying that I have the power to change anything. Neither do you or anyone else in this place or in this world. But God does. And it is our responsibility to keep pointing each other—Black, white, brown, yellow, and otherwise—to Him and His Word!"

"Alleluias" and "Glory be's" would ring out every week, but people didn't really want to hear that. They wanted something or someone to blame for the problems we all faced. Racism. *Right?* Inequality. *Right?* A history of selfishness and greed. *Right?* Fact is, it's easier to accept that we have no control over our problems than to face them, head on.

Every day was a battle. Every sermon, a gut-wrenching desire to try and communicate the differences between social justice and gospel justice. God wants His people to live together, as one, but we have to fix our eyes on Him before we can hope to fix one other.

Sandra and I fell victim to the belief that social justice was the answer more times than I can count: *If I pay their electric bill, maybe they'll see that as the love of Jesus and follow me to church.*

Nope. They got relief, not help. And that was the back and forth we, as a church, were dealing with now that "reconciliation" was a core value of Madison Square. Of course we should meet the needs of those who are hurting, needy, and less fortunate in our community, but we cannot forget about what they *need.*

I was developing a deep love for my people—Black people— during this time. I was starting to understand at a deep level that my life of loneliness and heartache, fatherlessness and my desperate search for love and community, was leading me to empathy. I felt the plight of the people around me at a deep, agonizing level.

When people are in a desperate place, a hopeless place, a life-or-death place, there can be no version of God big enough to pull them out. That broke my heart.

❊   ❊   ❊

Even as I was struggling to understand how God was going to use me in the place He had called me, Madison Square was growing, and we were being forced to consider adding a fourth service to our already exhausting schedule. Pastor Dave called me to his office where several members of the leadership team were waiting. "We'd like to offer you your own church site, Pastor Hardy. The details are still being worked out, but you'll pastor your own congregation. Two services a week."

I was numb; neither excited nor disappointed. I didn't know what to think or how to feel. I just stood there, my mouth unable to move and my eyes unable to blink. "I don't understand," I finally spoke. "Are you asking me to leave Madison Square?" An elder, a white man, stepped forward to explain: "We're not asking you to leave Madison," he said. "We're asking you to continue to grow it. You have a special message and a committed following, and we think you can build that following at a special and specific location, right up the street."

He was referring to Ford Elementary School. They said they were thinking about calling it "Madison at the Ford," and they wanted me to build it.

After talking about this new opportunity with Sandra, we agreed that this could be a good thing for our ministry. "We can be the church for the people around here that don't feel comfortable at Madison Square. It will be a safe place for the inner city."

Less than a month later, we had our first service at The Ford. More than a hundred people showed up. Ninety of them were white. I was humbled and honored, but as I looked out at the people I was serving—the people who were serving me by becoming a part of the church—my heart broke even more. Everyone there had been affected by my story over the past few years, but none of them understood it. None of them lived it. The people who were living my story were still outside. Still out on the street. Still searching for something they could not see.

There is a constant yearning and groaning that happens "out

there." A groaning we cannot hear when we are comfortably inside the walls of a church thanking God for His blessings on our lives. Out there, there is a groaning for belonging. A groaning for rest. A groaning for a Father.

My own fatherlessness hung around my neck like an albatross, a punishment for the sins of my childhood. I started a men's ministry and invited everyone I could find—homeless, drunks, men from all over the city, young and old. We met on Thursday nights at The Ford. The overarching message was that grace exists, redemption is real, and that forgiveness comes easy from the Father who loves us and wants the best for us. We are called, as men, to be leaders. To lead our families and be the head of the household. That's where healing begins in the family, and that is where healing will continue in our own lives. If we want a better world for ourselves and the people we love, God says that we have to lead.

After the first meeting, which was attended by approximately twenty-five white members of the church, three Black members, and a handful of walk-ins and passersby who saw the lights on and hoped for a cup of hot chocolate, I was approached by three elders.

"We have a problem," one of them said, motioning for me to sit. Another continued his thought, "Yeah. We're not sure about what you were saying tonight."

"I don't understand. What did I say?"

"You said that men are called to be leaders. I thought your whole message was that we are all the same. Why would you exclude the women?"

I laughed and tried to explain.

"My wife is a deacon," the third man interrupted. "Are you saying she can't serve others?"

"No, sir. That's not what I am saying at all. You see, we have a problem in this community, in the Black community, especially, where men are not fulfilling their God-given duty ..."

I was interrupted again. "So, it's a Black thing?" The first man was getting elevated. "I thought we were past that, Alton!"

Before I had an opportunity to try and convince these men that I wasn't taking a stand against women or whites, they all got up and left, making it clear they would not be back.

I sat in that room for over an hour, trying to make sense of what had just happened. Of course I didn't have anything against women. The women in my life had led me to great discovery and understanding of grace and love. But it wasn't until I began to truly see my community and look at them through the lens of my own experience that I began to see the void of strong, godly men.

Ninety percent of the issues I was seeing in our community were directly related to or caused by men who were not present. Angry, abusive, selfish, and lost ... men.

This call for Black men to step up and lead became more than a priority for me; it was a crusade. God was working on my own heart and allowing me to see that the fatherlessness in my life did not define or represent His presence in my life.

I was on a mission.

I decided then and there that I was no longer going to preach about race. Not at all. I simply wanted to do gospel ministry among the poor Blacks—the urban poor—who so desperately needed hope—for themselves, their families, and their futures.

The men's ministry only met a few more times, and the attendance was fewer and fewer each time, but "Urban Hope" became a message at the core of every sermon I gave. I was met with pushback almost every week. It became more and more difficult to hear the "amens" and "alleluias," and I was getting worn down by the blank faces that stared back at me from the congregation.

One Sunday, Louise Parker, a woman who had been described many times as "a great woman of prayer" came to me after the service and took my hand. "God is using you, Pastor Alton. And He is going to continue to use you to do great things for His Kingdom. But He is going to move you far, far away from here. When that time comes, don't argue it. Don't resist. God has a plan for you, but it's not here." I was not encouraged by her encouragement. I was devastated.

How could she say such a thing?
Was she being kind, or cruel?

*   *   *

Not everyone was put off by the Urban Hope message. Pastor Dave believed wholeheartedly with the vision. In fact, he had been working behind the scenes to grow the idea. He wanted to help create a gospel-centered ministry that would help my people—the downtrodden inner-city communities around Grand Rapids— understand their worth and value in the eyes of God.

A wealthy man at Madison Square named Ed DeVries owned a 73,000-square-foot building in the area and was considering donating the deed to Madison Square for the development of Urban Hope. We had dreams of building a church, a school, a workforce development facility, a working kitchen, a gymnasium, and more into this massive space. We began meeting multiple times a week to discuss how this new development might benefit thousands of people in our community.

My preaching took a turn. My enthusiasm was back with the excitement of what God was doing to change hearts and minds.

Even the naysayers and dissenters from months before were returning and hanging on every word that God was giving me to share each week.

And they were giving, too! The coffers were overflowing every week, and we were beginning to make this far-fetched dream a reality with every passing day.

Pastor Dave called me to his office on a Friday afternoon. Just like before, he was surrounded by smiling leadership and elders who welcomed me in with locker room enthusiasm. "Alton, we are fully funded. Urban Hope is going to happen, and you are the leader we need to make it go. Are you ready?"

I was overwhelmed. I started to laugh and cry at the same time. I couldn't believe the goodness and grace of God. Even after all He had brought me through and taught me over the last decade. I still couldn't believe it.

"We just need to figure out how to marry your agenda with our philosophy, and we'll be off to the races."

I sobered up immediately from my elation and questioned what had just been said.

"Well, you know," an elder from the back of the room spoke up. "You just need to stop with the men-only talk. You just stick to the race stuff and reconciliation and all that, and everything will be great."

I almost fell down.

I stumbled backward and then leaned in. "Do you really think I am pushing an agenda here? My agenda? This has nothing to do with me. This is God's agenda. And I have never said one discriminating thing about women. Quite the opposite. I just want to help grow strong, Black men who can take care of their responsibilities!" I was furious and heartbroken at the same time.

How could they not get it?

How could they not see?

After a few others tried to speak up, Pastor Dave abruptly ended the meeting and sent everyone home. He said we would meet again the following week to hash out a few more details.

2010

* * *

Two days after the meeting in Dave's office, I gave a sermon entitled "A Good Work" from Philippians 1:6.

"He who began a good work in you will bring it to completion at the day of Jesus Christ."

On Monday morning, with the blessing of my wife, a godly and dedicated believer in God's ultimate plan for Urban Hope, I resigned from Madison Church.

"The Lord gave you this vision, Alton. Now give it back to Him."

She was right. Was I willing to go halfway and receive the glory for this new, beautiful building and the potential good that it would do in our community, or was I committed to helping God fulfill Urban Hope? To enter into the inner city where people have been lied to and taught to believe the lies that they are not worthy or capable or made in the image of God. Sandra looked at me intently, and said, "You have the complete and total power of Jesus within you. Just follow Him, and I will follow you."

For years, God had been showing me that He could use my story and my circumstances to lead others to Him, that my fatherlessness could be an encouragement to those who desperately needed a Father. I had been hopeless for most of my life. I didn't understand that I had meaning and purpose. But when I found it, and God finally found me, I knew that I would go through hell if I had to in order to get to the place He called me to serve. To finally reach the Promised Land that I could not see.

It didn't take long for me to become one of the most reviled people in Madison. According to most, I was ungrateful, conceited, selfish, and unwilling to cooperate with the philosophies and theologies of Madison Square. I was shunned and deeply depressed for months. I questioned my decision to leave. I questioned God. I even questioned Sandra for agreeing to let me resign.

* * *

A few years earlier, back in 2006, I had attended a seminar in Detroit that was orchestrated by the DeVos Urban Leadership Initiative. It was an incredible three days that served as a master class in urban leadership. I learned so much about the inner workings of the inner city, and I met many extremely smart and dedicated individuals while I was there, including Ron Carter, who served as the executive director of the Initiative. The two of us became fast friends.

I was humbled and amazed by Ron's interest in me and what I was doing in Madison at the time. He surprised me over and over with his enthusiasm for my vision for race relations and gospel reconciliation in Grand Rapids. We promised to keep in touch and had several meaningful phone conversations over the next few years, but I was still surprised to get his call six months after I resigned at Madison Square.

I was not in a good place when the phone rang. I spent most of my days wallowing on the couch or sitting in a dark room questioning God's providence. I was in the middle of a full-on meltdown when I answered the phone with a huff.

"Alton! Is that you? It's Ron Carter, brother. How are you?"

He had to ask that question.

I wasn't prepared to get into what was actually happening with me, so I simply responded, "I'm good, Ron. Now might not be the best ti—" He interrupted.

"Listen, I want to introduce you to someone. I've been singing your praises, brother, and there are some folks down here who'd like to talk to you. What are you up to these days? How's Madison?"

He was talking so fast, I couldn't get a word in. "Good. Great. It's …" He started again: "You've got to talk to these guys, buddy. I've told them all about you. They want to start a church down here in Alabama, and you're perfect. Oh, and listen, that's not just me saying that. I've been talking to God about it, too!" He was laughing at this point, but kept going on and on about his friend, Jason.

Jason Williams grew up in inner-city DC. He had a hard life but had turned everything around a decade or so earlier. He was serving as the director of Urban Missions at a church near Birmingham.

Ron set up a call between me and Jason the next day, and we hit it off immediately. He was one of the friendliest brothers I had ever talked to. He was happy, funny, and throwing around slang as if he had been in my crew back in Louisville. It was one of the biggest shocks of my life to find out that Jason Williams is white!

I couldn't believe it.

He shared the vision that his church, Briarwood Presbyterian, had for their urban initiatives, and he asked me to share mine.

"Listen, dog," he got serious for a minute. "We need somebody like you to come help us get this city back on track. Ron says great things about you, brother. You check every box, bro. What do you say? You wanna come down for a visit? Bring the fam. We'll have a good time."

A week later, Sandra and I were on a plane to Birmingham. Jeremiah stayed in Grand Rapids with some of Sandra's friends, so we were able to use the time we had together to wonder, dream, and pray. Jason picked us up from the airport in his Cadillac Escalade, and he was everything I had imagined. He was wearing extra large basketball shorts that reached past his knees, and a Chicago Bulls T-shirt that had "World Champions, 1993" printed across the front. He didn't stop talking for the entire three days we were with him. His enthusiasm was contagious, and I couldn't help but to share in his excitement about us being there.

I had never been to Birmingham. I spent the first eleven years of my life ninety miles from there, but I couldn't have ever imagined how beautiful it actually was. Briarwood sits just south of the city, surrounded by trees and big, beautiful neighborhoods full of huge houses—unlike anything anywhere close to where we came from. The church itself is enormous. I had never seen or stepped foot into any place like it. But that's not where we were headed. Jason drove us to Fairfield, a city in western Jefferson County, just barely within the Birmingham Metropolitan Area.

Fairfield was founded in 1910, when the guest speaker at the ceremony was former President Theodore Roosevelt. It must have been a wonderful time!

But the next hundred years were not kind to Fairfield. Not at all. It became a desperate and desolate place with a population that consisted of 95 percent Blacks and only 2 percent whites.

"This is a place in need of Urban Hope," Jason said as he looked at me over his big aviator sunglasses and smiled.

The next two and a half days were packed with meetings, guided tours, prayer, and vision-casting. Every person I met was fascinated as I discussed my history, my goals, and my desire to bring the hope of Jesus to the inner city. I felt like we were being asked to return home to a place and to a family we had never known.

And then, on August 8, 2012, my forty-sixth birthday, we did.

PART FIVE
URBAN HOPE

It was only 94 degrees that day, but I'll never forget the look Sandra gave me as we exited the air-conditioned moving truck and stepped into the dog days of central Alabama. There was an earnestness in her eyes, as if to say, "It's not too late. We can still go back. Maybe we heard Him wrong. Surely, God doesn't want us *here*." Even though I had grown up in the South, I had been out of it just long enough to forget the absolute swelter that we had just devoted the rest of our lives to.

The heat wasn't the only thing that would test us after our move South. Everything was new. Everything was different. Not to mention, we took a loss on the sale of our house in Grand Rapids and left the only home Sandra and Jeremiah had ever known with nothing but what we were able to fit in our tiny U-Haul.

Birmingham, Alabama, is nowhere near—literally and figuratively—everything Sandra had built for herself and for our family in Michigan.

My thoughts echoed the words I could read on my wife's face and in her teary eyes:

What. Have. I. Done?

* * *

Before I could officially be considered as a pastor in the PCA Church, I had to meet various requirements as mandated by the

Presbyterian Church in America Book of Church Order. Most of the requirements were easy, but Licensure and Ordination almost granted Sandra's wish to run back to a more temperate fall. My head was spinning as I read:

> *The exam consists of a statement regarding Christian experi ence and calling and a written or oral exam on the Westminster standards, practical knowledge of the Bible, and a basic knowledge of the PCA's Book of Church Order, as well as the submission and presentation of a written sermon on an assigned passage of Scripture.*

All of those requirements were doable. I had been required to memorize Scripture before, I was familiar with many of the Church's standards, and I could certainly preach a sermon on an assigned topic. I had been taking direction from Pastor Dave for years. But that wasn't all. There were tests. So many tests.

> *The candidate must then be examined on his experiential religion, personal character, and family management, knowledge of Greek and Hebrew, Bible content, theology, the Sacraments, church history, the history of the PCA, and the principles and rules of the government and discipline of the church. He must also prepare a thesis on an assigned theological topic and prepare and preach an exegetical sermon requiring knowledge of the original languages.*

Suddenly, I was the fatherless little boy from Sardis again—shoeless, shirtless, lost, and scared. I was the poor kid in Newburg. The frightened, lost, lonely, and homeless teenager in Grand Rapids. The failure at Alpena. The failure at marriage. The failure at Madison Church.

I failed over and over again.

All I wanted to do was share the gospel to the inner city and to the communities I had been called to serve. All I wanted to do was lead conversations around unity and reconciliation. All I wanted to do was to give others a glimpse of the hope that comes from knowing and following Jesus. And I kept being told, "No. No. No."

You're not good enough. You're not smart enough. You haven't studied enough. You don't know enough. You. Are. Not. Enough.

At one point, after another failed attempt at a passing grade, one of the elders at the church tried to console me: "Don't worry about it, son," he said. "I think this is why the PCA doesn't have very many Black pastors. These tests are really hard."

December 2012

*   *   *

I called Jason Williams, unable to hold back tears, and told him that I was done. I wasn't going to be able to help Briarwood Presbyterian Church build a ministry in Fairfield.

I failed. Again.

"Urban Hope might happen," I said, "but it's going to be without me." I was crying. "I'm too tired. I'm beat, man. I've got to go home."

There was silence on the other end of the phone, and then, finally, an exhale. "That's crap," he said casually. I was stunned.

"That's crap, and you know it, Alton. I know you are tired, brother, but you are *not* beat." His voice was getting louder. "Your whole life has been leading up to this! You have been created and called *for such a time as this*, bro."

Even with his encouragement, I was overwhelmed to the point of paralysis. I couldn't sleep. I couldn't eat. I couldn't focus on anything other than the life I had left in Grand Rapids.

If I had just agreed to do whatever Madison told me to do, I would be in charge of a thriving ministry right now. I would have a huge building, a staff, and a church committed to helping the people in their community.

I had nothing in Fairfield. No ministry. No church. No support. Just a constant reminder that I didn't have what it takes to lead people—Black or white.

Jason gave me a couple of weeks to think about my decision before it was final. I was so scared. Sandra wanted to support me, but she didn't know how. I spent hours each day curled up on the couch, or never even leaving my bedroom. I was mad at God. He had abandoned me. Again.

The only wish I had for my life was that He could use me, and He was nowhere to be found. I had to let Jason know my answer on January 1.

It was raining on New Year's Eve. Sandra and Jeremiah were at the mall, and I was still shut down; frozen by fear, uncertainty, and a nagging feeling that God was trying to tell me something. I called out: *Let me hear from you, Lord! Show me yourself! Tell me what I am supposed to do! Are you even there? Do you even care?*

Sandra had given me an iPad for Christmas, and I hadn't even taken it out of the package. The silence in my bedroom was excruciating, so I walked over and unboxed the gift. Perhaps God would send me Scripture to look up, a parable or something.

I typed the letters "P.C.A." into the search screen and waited for the results:

> "Principal component analysis …"
> "Presbyterian Church in America"
> "The Porsche Club of America"
> "Parcel Corporation of America"

Parcel Corporation of America? PCA? I clicked on the blue line of words and was immediately taken to the website of PCA: "Custom and bulk packaging products in Grand Rapids, Michigan …"

The iPad slowly slid out of my hands and onto the floor, and I followed, directly to my knees. God used one of the most painful moments of my life to not only remind me of where I had been, but to tell me that He had me exactly where I was supposed to be.

"I have you where I have you. I have orchestrated the good days and the bad days. I knew you before you were born. I saw this day before you did. I knew what I was going to use your story to do—for others … for you … and for my Kingdom.

Alton, this tapestry we are weaving together has mountaintops and valleys; dense woods and rivers; city streets and alleyways; people who look like you and people who do not. I know what the finished work looks like, and one day, you will, too. Just trust me."

* * *

I called Jason and told him that I had been wrong. I told him that whatever I had to do to pass the tests, I would do. For the next two weeks, I studied with a new energy. I was no longer afraid of failing. I expected to pass. I knew that it would happen. And it did. I passed all five tests with flying colors, and Urban Hope was born.

SUNDAY, NOON

*　*　*

Brothers and sisters, it has been ten years since God called us to Fairfield. We have spent a decade trying to help bring new life to that tired town, and it has not been easy.

Poverty and crime are still rampant there. It is a place still living with the ache of history. Most days, our work is humbling. Many days, it is heartbreaking.

But every day is a reminder of the goodness and grace of God.

He is doing miraculous things through His people in the inner city. Lives are being changed, souls are being saved. And a community, once lost, is being found over and over again by people from all walks of life.

Back in the day, the Jim Crow system impacted everyone—from where and when and how Blacks and whites could come together, to how we all lived. Blacks were second class citizens, and whites, even if they wanted to, were not allowed to treat us any other way. Jim Crow was about complete and total separation—even in the church.

The manifold vision is a model of bringing God's people together— especially through the church. And He, too, will impact every aspect of life.

Urban Hope is a vehicle through which God is using His people to make this vision come to fruition. Not just for those of us in Fairfield, but for all of us. We're not there yet. We still have a long way to go. But that just means God is still writing our stories.

When Moses took the Jews out of Egypt, toward the Promised Land, they took the long way; the road less traveled, so to speak. Geographically, they could have gotten to Israel within a couple of weeks, but that's not the route they took. Why? Because God still had things to teach them before they got there. He was still writing their stories.

As lonely and scary and dangerous as the wilderness may be, God allows us to go there because it is in our desperate neediness that He prepares us for the story He is writing with our lives.

Sometimes, the long way makes us stronger because of our experiences; more mature and focused because of the adversities and atrocities we've faced; and eventually, more confident that it has been God who has been leading us the whole way.

One thing I've come to know and believe is that God has always been with me. I've been lonely most of my life, but I have never been alone.

* * *

There's an old Sam Cooke song that starts, "I was born by the river, in a little tent, oh, and just like the river, I've been running ever since ..." I've probably heard that song a thousand times throughout the years. I've even sung along to the lyrics, much to the chagrin of

*anyone within earshot. But I never paid attention
to the words until recently:*

*"I was born by the river
In a little tent
Oh, and just like the river, I've been running
Ever since."*

*Me. Alton Hardy. A fatherless, friendless fool; a stuttering,
stammering Black kid from Sardis. A poor, homeless young man by
way of Louisville and Grand Rapids; a man of God, finally arriving
in the place where He intends to use me for His glory. For such a
time as this.*

*It is His wisdom that allows all of us to arrive at this place—
wherever He has us—together.*

*Has there ever truly been a manifold of God's people—from every
race, color, tongue, and tribe—standing in the gospel, together?*

*Are you ready to stand together?
I ain't running no more.*

*"It's been a long, long time comin';
but I know a change 'gon come;
Oh, yes it will."*

*Hab mercy, y'all.
And amen.*

MANIFOLDVISION.ORG  URBANHOPECC.ORG

Q&A WITH ALTON

* * *

Q: OK, LET'S START AT THE END. CAN YOU EXPLAIN YOUR VISION FOR URBAN HOPE?

Gospel unity. Period. First and foremost, Urban Hope is a church-planting initiative that will put churches in the heart of the inner city. We've done that in Fairfield, and we will be using Urban Hope Community Church in Fairfield as a model for expansion to other areas. This is the manifold vision of God: to see people freed from bondage. Though the material and financial issues of the inner city are easy to see and tempting to focus on, there are deeper, spiritual issues that need to be addressed. Urban Hope wants to be a stabilizing presence in the inner city by investing in much-needed community development efforts. There is a dire need in these places for thriving churches where the gospel is preached, men are discipled to reach their God-given potential, and families can begin to thrive ... even in the neighborhoods that have been neglected for so long.

Q: WHY BIRMINGHAM?

Because Birmingham has long been known as the apex for racial divide in America. The manifold vision of God is just the opposite. The manifold is where Black people and white people and people of all walks of life come together "for such a time as this." The two most unlikely groups of God's people coming together to fulfill God's ultimate plan for His people. I believe God's plan for my life was to always come home, to come back to this place and share my story and show His ultimate power and grace. If God can do what He is doing in Birmingham, we know that He can do it in all places where there is divide—both geographically and in our hearts.

Q: WHERE CAN WE LEARN MORE ABOUT URBAN HOPE? HOW CAN OTHERS HELP?

The best place to learn about the vision is to visit manifoldvision. org. If you want to learn about our Urban Hope initiatives in Fairfield, visit UrbanHopeCC.org. The best way to help us complete the mission God has set before us is to pray. I believe that God will meet you in those prayers and guide your steps as we venture out together.

Q: OK, LET'S GO BACK TO THE BEGINNING. WHAT WAS THE MAIN THING MISSING IN YOUR LIFE WHEN YOU WERE GROWING UP IN SARDIS?

Looking back, I was always searching for meaning. Even as a five-year-old, I didn't know why I was on the earth. I had no sense of identity. No reason to be alive. I walked every day to try and find a reason to keep walking. Nature provided me comfort. It was always there, but it also represents diversity to me and all things becoming new. Every tree is not the same. Every flower is different. And even when I was very young, I was moved by the bigness of God's realm. That fascination persists today. He made it all.

Q: WHAT HAPPENED TO YOUR FRIENDS IN LOUISVILLE?

I still connect with L.A. and Pooh from time to time. They know how important they were and are to my life. Most of my friends from Louisville ended up staying in Louisville and never really left that old neighborhood. I had very little contact with them before I landed in Birmingham, but over the past decade I have felt the desire to reconnect with them. I loved those guys and they loved me. They were the first real community I ever had, and they helped define who I am. But now I can see clearly why God removed me from that place. Our paths have gone in different directions. While I still love and appreciate those people, I think God was protecting me from some of the situations I would have been put in back in Louisville. He knew that I was not strong enough to live that life.

Q: WHAT KIND OF IMPACT HAVE THE WOMEN IN YOUR LIFE MADE ON YOU?

The women who are represented in this book: my mother, Toni, Lucille, Marylin, Sandra, and so many others, changed my life. They *saved* my life. They mean everything to me. And it is through them—these remarkable women—that I have been given a firsthand understanding of the great burden put on single mothers throughout our country and the world. All of these women impacted me more than I could have ever known or understood. They, more than anyone else in my life, made me who I am. They are strength and beauty and grit and love and light. All of them. God has used the women in my life to give me a perfect picture of His creation and how we are ALL created in the image of God Almighty. They have helped me to define the ministry I have been called to serve, and that is precisely why I want to help raise up strong *men* so that the burden of these remarkable women might be made light.

Q: TALK TO ME ABOUT YOUR "MOM," LUCILLE, IN GRAND RAPIDS.

Lucille is still alive and kicking. She is just as much of a spitfire at ninety-one years old as she was when I was in high school. Without Lucille coming into my life when she did, I do not think I would be alive today. God put her in my life at exactly the right time. She was tough. She was loving. She was God-fearing. And she taught me more about Jesus than most theologians ever have. She was a bright light at a very dark time, and she continues to shine to this day. I often think about how much God must love me to have given me my mom, Lucille.

Q: WHAT IS YOUR RELATIONSHIP WITH MARYLIN TODAY?

First and foremost, I want people to know that Marylin, which is not her real name, is not a bad person. She is no more broken than any one of us. The role she played in my life was vital to me becoming the man I am today. God used her to help reveal my own brokenness and neediness. She helped to reveal my need for a Father. I didn't know how to be a man when she needed a man. I didn't know how to be a father. I was a shell of myself when she needed strength. I was cold-hearted when she needed kindness. Since our divorce, Marylin and I have developed a mutual respect for one another. I consider her a friend. I am grateful for her. I thank God for her.

Q: THERE ARE SEVERAL MEN WHO PLAYED CRUCIAL ROLES IN YOUR STORY: BROTHERS, FRIENDS, AND FATHER FIGURES LIKE BOBBY CARR, ELMO, ARTHUR BAILEY, AND DAVE BEELEN. FOR OTHERS WHO MIGHT FEEL THE PAIN OF FATHERLESSNESS, WHAT ENCOURAGEMENT CAN YOU GIVE TO THEM BASED ON THE THINGS YOU'VE LEARNED FROM THE MEN IN YOUR LIFE?

The first encouragement I might give is to acknowledge at a heart level that there is a void. When we feel lonely and alone—especially with regard to our earthly fathers—that emptiness is there for a reason. Allow your desperate neediness to linger and then you will begin to understand why that void exists. All of those men have filled different voids my life, and it was only when I was able to sit in that pain of wanting that God revealed His love for me through those men. I clung to Elmo because he was strong. He was a disciplinarian; I was drawn to Bobby Carr because of how well he loved his family; Arthur was a great example of being a professional—doing what you say you will do, being organized, and setting goals; and Pastor Dave helped me to understand how God has specifically created me. How to love others as myself, and how to represent my family by first loving my heavenly Father, and then my wife. He taught me to fight for my heart.

Q: WHAT REALLY HAPPENED AT MADISON SQUARE CHRISTIAN REFORMED CHURCH IN GRAND RAPIDS?

Madison Square CRC is one of the greatest blessings in my life. I loved, and still love, the people there who helped shape me as a leader and man of God. I love the depth of their hearts and the motives behind their willingness and want to engage in hard things. While at Madison, my heart became broken for the inner city, and all of my own history came rushing in to remind me of the things most lacking in my own life growing up—the love and guidance of an earthly father, and the support of a thriving community. Fatherlessness is a plague among all people, but within the Black community especially. The absence of men in homes, and the absence of fathers in children's lives, is one of the greatest contributors to most of the many issues facing the inner city. I wanted to help build up young men in families. I wanted to focus my ministry efforts on helping Black men take ownership of their identity as beloved sons of God, and as the leaders they are created to be. Madison CRC has an egalitarian theological and worldview, which contradicted my vision to undergird the roles of men. My decision to leave Madison was not based on the issues of reconciliation or the inequity among races. It was because I felt God calling me to the deeper, more insidious issue of fatherlessness.

Q: WHY IS IT IMPORTANT TO YOU TO FOCUS ON BUILDING UP MEN?

There are literally thousands of statistics that prove how important men are to our society. There are certainly just as many that speak to the importance of women, but research shows when a child is raised in a father-absent home, they are four times at greater risk to live in poverty, more likely to go to prison, commit a crime, face abuse and neglect, and more likely to abuse drugs and alcohol. Teen pregnancies are increased sevenfold, and those children are two times more likely to drop out of school. These are all issues that plague our inner-cities, and I believe that God has called me to help build up young men so that they can begin to develop healthy relationships, build strong family units, and help to heal our broken communities. Strong, God-fearing men make better husbands and fathers, and better husbands and fathers can help bring about the change we really need in our homes, neighborhoods, cities, nation, and world.

Q: WHAT ARE YOUR CHILDREN UP TO THESE DAYS?

Amaad works for the NAACP in Grand Rapids. He is a huge-hearted young man who believes that he is going to change the world, and I believe that, too. He is a talented musician and extremely involved with the Democratic Party in Michigan.

Jalen is a gorgeous, young businesswoman who lives in Atlanta, Georgia, with my beautiful grandson, Karter.

Jeremiah works for Chick-fil-A, Inc. and helps with the grand openings of their new restaurants, which allows him to travel the country and use his affable, outgoing personality to build relationships all over the world.

Q: WHY WAS IT IMPORTANT TO YOU TO TELL YOUR STORY?

That is an important question. The obvious answer is that God writes our stories, and I believe that there are certain stories He intends to magnify in order to bring attention back to Himself. I believe that my story is a powerful reminder that reconciliation and healing comes through Him and Him only. My story is just one example of how God can use the broken and the brokenhearted, but I believe that He has called me to lean into the hope that only He can give.

Q: WHAT MAKES YOUR STORY SPECIAL?

My story is only special because of Jesus Christ, but it is *truly* special because of Him. He orchestrated all of my days—the good and the bad—and I believe He intends to use the experiences of my life to bring about unity like we've never known. He has the Power to change everything toward His will any time He wants, but He chooses His children to play the roles He has created for the stories He wants told. *That's* special.

ALTON HARDY

* * *

First, I want to thank the Lord, God who created me and knew me before I was formed in my mother's womb. He numbered all my days and saw them before one of them came to be.

Thank you Sandra, my wife, who has brought much joy into my life.

Thank you, Greg Mixon, for being the best friend and lawyer in the world. Thank you for making this book a reality and one who saw this before I would come to believe it.

Thank you, Billy Ivey, for your willingness and gracious heart to hear very difficult and hard stories of my life and then work through all the emotions of it and put it on paper for others to read it with their hearts.

Thank you for Small Stories investors who invested in Billy, therefore allowing for this story to be told to the world.

Thank you for all the different individuals in this book who God allowed me to meet and interact with in this short vapor of a life. Your interactions with me, good or bad, helped shape me to be the man I am today.

Special thanks to the Pastor Dave Beelen, Arthur Bailey, Ron Carter, Lucille Barnes, Elmo and Clarence Carlisle, Beth Drennen, and the Manifold Vision team of advisors.

BILLY IVEY

* * *

Thank you, Lord—for loving us in spite of us; for being in control even when we fail to see your hand at work. Even when the road is long. Even in the dark.

Thank you for the words.

Thank you, Alton. I love you, brother, and I am forever grateful that you trusted me to tell your story. You've changed my life.

Thank you, Greg Mixon, for being faithful; for your wisdom; for your love; for your vision to see the world-changing potential of small stories. Thank you, Jon. Thank you, Tony Jones, for loving me, but loving Jesus even more. Thank you Beth and Ward Drennen, for your constant support and encouragement.

Thank you, Bethany, my heart. Thank you, Anna Beth, for always being willing to read what I write, and for always loving my words, even when they aren't right. Thank you, Ben, for reminding me to smile. Merrie Cannon, for always smiling. Abe, for always interrupting with your creativity and wonder. Quinn, for always asking questions that I can't answer. You people are my everything.

Thank you to Mary Virginia and Chet Frist for your radical hospitality.

Thanks to Mandy and Jason Sears for your love of me and mine; for giving me the space where I found most of the words in this book.

Special thanks to Jean and Jerry Eickhoff, Leonard Lee, Aaron Spigner, Eric Chapman, Josh Moore, James Harris, Ryan Harrison, Michael Southerland, Chad Gibbs, Becky Philpott, and so many others who have inspired and enabled me more than you can know.

Thanks to David Ryan Harris, the Avett Brothers, Bob Schneider, Dawes, David Ramirez, 2Pac, Rachmaninoff, and Braves broadcasters, Ben Ingram and Joe Simpson for serving as the soundtrack to this story.

And, finally, thanks to Edgar's Bakery, O'Henry's Coffeehouse, East 59 Cafe, and various Starbucks locations for the free internet, wobbly tables, caffeine, and breakfast foods.

ABOUT THE AUTHORS

ALTON HARDY is an ordained teaching elder of the Presbyterian Church in America (PCA). Alton is the pastor and founder of Urban Hope Community Church, co-founder of Urban Hope Development, and the visionary behind the Urban Hope Leadership Initiative. He and his wife, Sandra, live in Fairfield, Alabama and are passionate about addressing conditions facing urban communities and living out true gospel reconciliation.

BILLY IVEY is a writer and creative director, and co-founder of Small Stories Studio in Birmingham, Alabama. He earned his BA in English Literature from Samford University, and enjoyed a long career in advertising before starting Small Stories. He lives outside of Birmingham with his wife, Bethany, and a varying number of their five children. Billy's first book, *A Sea Between Us* (Tyndale, 2022) is available wherever great books are sold.

www.ingramcontent.com/pod-product-compliance
Lightning Source LLC
Chambersburg PA
CBHW031125130726
47988CB00006B/2223